POWERFUL MATE SYNDROME

POWERFUL
MATE
SYNDROME

RECLAIMING YOUR STRENGTH AND

PURPOSE WHEN YOUR PARTNER

IS THE STAR OF THE RELATIONSHIP

ANGELA WILDER

ST. MARTIN'S PRESS ❦ NEW YORK

www.stmartins.com

ISBN 0-312-33344-7
EAN 978-0312-33344-7

First Edition: October 2004

10 9 8 7 6 5 4 3 2 1

TO MY BELOVED mother, Oshia Brown Reid, without whose love and support I would not have been able to write this book. You pulled up stakes in North Carolina, leaving behind family, friends, a beautiful home, and everything that was familiar, and came to California because I needed you. Thank you for every meal you cooked, every load of laundry you did, the chauffeuring of my girls to everything from soccer practice to bat mitzvahs to doctor's appointments. But most of all, thank you for listening to my ranting and raving when I felt overwhelmed, for making me laugh when I wanted to cry, and for always being available at a moment's notice. When others doubted me, you believed in me—even when I didn't believe in myself. Words are inadequate to express how much I love you and how much you mean to me. Thank you.

To my beloved father, Timothy Wilder. I thank you for teaching me the importance of dreams, the value of education, and the power in persevering. Thank you for your love and encouragement through the years. I want you to know that during this entire process I have kept in the forefront of my thoughts something that you often say: "The view never changes unless you're the lead cow." Thank you for your warm Southern witticism. It buoys me when my life gets heavy. I love you.

To my grandmother, Wessye Taylor Brown, who was light years ahead of her time. You instilled in me a love of both the written and the spoken word, Sunday morning news shows, professional sports, and browsing in thrift shops. Your grace, intellectual prowess, sharp wit, biting humor, and sheer determination were such gifts in my life. I wish you could be here to celebrate this tremendous accomplishment with me but I know that you've been here in spirit every step of the way.

And last but not least, to my amazing daughters, Sable and Sierra. Thank you for your enthusiasm and support from the day I wrote the first sentence of this book. Your willingness to give up weekends and holidays that I had to spend at my desk writing and your cooperation by finding ways to entertain yourselves at home meant more to me than you'll ever know. Thank you for the neck, hand, and foot massages you gave me when I became so fatigued that I thought I would collapse. You two held me up when I needed it—and you kept me anchored when I needed it. I am privileged to be your mother. You are awesome and I love you infinitely! Just please don't make me any more of those "everything that's in the pantry" muffins!

All my love,
Your daughter, granddaughter, and mother, Angela

CONTENTS

AUTHOR'S NOTE

NOTHING I HAVE written in this book is intended to cause hurt or harm to anyone, particularly my former husband, James Worthy. My life with James spanned two decades, and in spite of our divorce there is a rich shared history between us. Our relationship, while terminated as husband and wife, was the living laboratory from which this book was born. Writing this book has given me the opportunity to realize that there is always room for greater understanding and, thus, forgiveness. This realization is particularly poignant in light of the fact that we are lifetime parenting partners to our extraordinary daughters, Sierra and Sable.

In that same vein, because I wanted to ensure the confidentiality of everyone whose cases or experiences I have discussed in this book, all names and identifying details have been changed. Additionally, it is important to acknowledge here that Powerful Mate Syndrome is neither an exclusively female nor heterosexual issue. It is a relationship issue and either partner, regardless of gender or the couple's sexual orientation, can be affected. I used the pronoun *she* more often than *he* simply to avoid making the text unwieldy. Please know that it was not done to render invisible anyone who lives in the shadow of a powerful mate.

Who looks outside, dreams; who looks inside, awakes.
—CARL JUNG

POWERFUL MATE SYNDROME

INTRODUCTION

ALL OF US, at one time or another in our lives, have been told, "Be careful what you wish for because you just might get it." I certainly heard that message. Too bad I didn't pay attention. When I said "I do" to my fairy-tale prince, I had no idea that I was simultaneously agreeing to a long and painful process of losing my identity. I had no idea that I was plunging myself headlong into Powerful Mate Syndrome. After all, my husband James was at the top of his field (professional basketball). He was strong, handsome, and respected and admired the world over—and he professed his undying love for me. That's all that was on my mind. Wouldn't our marrriage bring me a greater sense of my own personal power, support for my goals, joy like I had never known, and also form the basis of a formidable, life-long partnership? The short answer is no. In fact, no one can perform that kind of miracle in anyone else's life. But I didn't know that. I didn't know that my betrothal was the beginning of my betrayal—not his betrayal of me but my

1

betrayal of myself. My marriage to James sent me on a downward spiral psychologically, emotionally, spiritually, and even, in some ways, physically.

Like so many girls growing up in this culture, my dangerous wish was to meet my prince, fall madly in love, marry him, and live happily ever after—and oh, let's not forget the extravagant wedding gown, awe-inspiring ceremony, and dream honeymoon. Of course, not every woman dreams of marrying a sports star as I did, but the Cinderella fantasy still runs strong. We think that by marrying a star—whatever kind of star we wish for—our dreams will come true.

This myth is perpetuated not only by our friends and family but by countless books, magazines, and television shows, including *Who Wants to Marry a Millionaire, The Bachelor,* and *The Bachelorette,* which gave us the modern version of the Cinderella story featuring Trista and Ryan. On a conscious level we may not be aware of how fully we have integrated this fairy tale into our collective unconscious, but the archetype of the powerful hero who comes to the rescue of the "damsel in distress" is alive and well in the psyches of pretty much every woman I know.

Let's get this straight once and for all. Cinderella is a myth. There are no guarantees of "happily ever after" even if you do marry the prince. A happy marriage is based on hard work, not hope; it takes common sense and commitment. Cinderella and the prince get to live happily ever after in our imaginations because the beginning of their life together is also **THE END.** We never get to "ever after"! It's not part of the story. No, Cinderella never had to deal with the challenges of *living* with her prince, and we never had to witness her struggle to maintain her own integrity and identity in the shadows of power.

Too bad I didn't know that. My Cinderella fantasy lasted for years. For years I clung to the fantasy of being a helpless princess who would be taken care of by my omnipotent prince. That fantasy kept me from realizing that there is a world of difference between being cared *for* and being taken care *of.* A healthy marriage is all about being cared for, allowing each other room for independence, intellectual growth, and emotional expansion. Being taken care of, on the other hand, fosters dependency, intellectual atrophy, limited life experiences, and stifled creativity; it certainly does not cultivate self-reliance. When we make our mates our gods we end up worshipping them and lose sight and sense of ourselves. In my marriage to James, I sacrificed my own career ambitions. I came to rely on my husband to validate me as a person. I stopped voicing my own opinions on things that mattered to both of us, and I did not believe that I had the right to "complain." In short, I became a glamorous appendage to a powerful man.

Believe me, I didn't consciously choose to become the pitiful creature that I evolved into. My lack of knowledge about the reality of marriage, my denial of my need for achievement and acknowledgement in my own right, my naiveté about the temptations in the world of professional sports, my lack of experience with money, and my failure to think about life after James's career ended all had deleterious effects on me, my former husband, and our marriage. My marriage didn't have to be that way, and neither does yours.

Ironically, when I was growing up, every woman in my life worked outside the home. None of my friends had moms who stayed at home. I thought that was the way it was supposed to be. Every woman whom I considered a role model, from my grandmothers to my mom to Barbara Jordan, the erudite Texas congresswoman who served from the mid-1960s to the late 1970s, and even the fictitious Mary Richards on *Mary Tyler Moore*, was a working woman. I never imagined that my life would be any different. I knew from the time I was ten years old that I wanted to have a career that afforded me the opportunity to do three things: First, I wanted to meet new people every day; second, I wanted to learn something new every day; third, I wanted to work in television journalism.

I was probably the only child in my fifth grade class who went home and watched the Watergate hearings every day. I found them fascinating and entertaining. Watching those hearings gave me great respect for Barbara Jordan. Her eloquence, her laser-sharp recitation of passages from the Constitution and Bible verses, and the hypnotic cadence of her speech mesmerized me. She and Barbara Walters were the two famous women whom I idolized and wanted to emulate. Through high school and college I carried my dreams of being like "the two Barbaras." I still had those dreams when I came to Los Angeles to begin my life as James's wife.

Los Angeles was the Promised Land for James. He was firmly ensconced in his role as a starting forward with the Lakers. He was manifesting his childhood dreams of success, fame, and fortune that first came to him as he played at the Boys and Girls Club in Gastonia, North Carolina. I reveled in his success, too. It was a joy to watch his transformation from basketball apprentice to master of the hoop. In my eyes, there was no one who played better at his position than James. He was simply the best.

On the other hand, Los Angeles proved not as instantly promising for me. Unlike James's job as the member of a team where most career-related issues are planned and well-defined—practice schedules, travel itineraries, and fitness regimens—for me there was no clear path to accomplishing my career goals. Should I go to UCLA and study broadcast journalism, try to sign with a modeling agency, enroll in a commercial workshop, or take some acting classes? I had landed a Pepsi commercial while I was still in Chapel Hill, which had enabled me to join the Screen Actors Guild even before I moved to Los Angeles. I thought that acting classes might be the place to start. Even though I had no intentions of being an actress per se, I knew that getting into a class where I'd have to get up in front of other people and perform would be good for me, no matter what I did in my career.

I enrolled in a scene study class and a commercial workshop. The classes met at night, which meant that I would sometimes miss James's games. That was no big deal. I didn't believe that he needed me to be at every game. After all, he'd spent two seasons playing in Los Angeles while I was still in Chapel Hill. I plodded along, always looking for the opportunity that would catapult me into the working world—the world in which I knew I belonged.

Now I'm not saying that every woman needs to work outside the home to feel whole and fulfilled. If being a stay-at-home mom is your calling, then that is what you should do. But that doesn't mean that you can't take a vacation alone to

Paris and study all the architecture that you've longed to see since you were an art history student in college. More and more women are starting their own businesses right from their homes. Do it if that's what calls you! This is not about being rich, famous, or bigger than your partner. It is about doing whatever makes you feel whole, challenged, and validated. It's about giving birth to your dream and doing what it takes to nurture it, grow it, and have it give something back to you.

I never thought I'd hidden my intention to pursue a career in television from James. He knew I loved being in front of people. He'd seen me in front of twenty thousand fans every weekend while I was a cheerleader at Carolina. I had even spoken of trying to go to New York to pursue my goals before we got married. I thought we had a meeting of the minds, that we would both strive to be the best we could be in our chosen fields of endeavor. Before I got married that was a realistic goal. After I got married, even that became a distant fantasy.

For a woman who grows up believing in the Cinderella story, the ultimate coup is to marry the prince who can make it so that she does not have to work outside the home. He provides for her every need, want, and wish. He is her sun and moon, her god, her protector, her lover and friend. Heck, with a catch like that she doesn't need anyone else in her life. For me, the ultimate coup truly would have been a happy marriage and a fulfilling and challenging life outside of that marriage. But sometime shortly after I got married, the adventurous and independent woman that I was during my teens and in college got suppressed. Oh yes, amid great fanfare and anticipation I became Mrs. James Worthy—and

I lost my way. I cannot pinpoint the moment in time that I went AWOL, but I know that it mysteriously happened shortly after I took those vows. I enthroned him as the king of my world and, rather than doing what it took to be a powerful queen, I assumed the role as the king's subject. There was an obvious imbalance in the power department of our relationship. He had ninety-nine percent of it; I had the rest.

Why? Because I gave it to him. I became an appendage of James, as opposed to being my own person. You see, "appendages" no longer give their own goals priority status. Instead, they become complicit in their own invisibility.

I've know too many women like me, who have abandoned their own dreams in favor of helping their man achieve his. Such is the case with a woman who desires to be a medical doctor herself but then marries another medical student and decides to take a job "just for a while," in order to help him attain his goal, in the belief that someday he will return the gesture and help her realize hers. But "someday" never comes. By the time it gets around to being "her turn," if they are even still together, there are often children in the picture, which requires a new set of responsibilities, the lion's share of which typically fall to her.

In some cases, a woman will give up the pursuit of her dreams so as not to draw attention away from her partner. Rather than subscribing to the belief that the spotlight is large enough to encompass both of them, she exits stage left while he takes his place at center stage. Oftentimes a man feels threatened by his spouse's success and either consciously or subconsciously attempts to quash it. It is amazing how a man who is powerful out in the world, either through his career achievements, family legacy, or wealth, can become absolutely terrified by the prospect of his wife creating her own power base, being able to take care of herself, and having a life that revolves around more than him.

I began to live an almost split existence. One part of me lived in denial so that I could push down the sadness and rage that I felt over becoming, for all intents and purposes, a servant. The denial also helped me adopt the belief that it would be enough to live in the reflected glory of James's career. My life had become about living vicariously through him. It's hard to become the next Barbara Walters when you're at home doing a bad impression of a Happy Homemaker.

The most baffling thing about our situation was that I don't even know exactly when the shift in our roles took place. It wasn't as though there was a sudden change in my actions or thoughts. I didn't wake up one day and declare, "Today I am going to become subordinate, complacent, weak, and unfocused," but that is exactly what happened. I had gotten myself into quite a mess, and it would be up to me to get myself out of it. I had no clue at the time that eventually I would have to get out of that relationship in order to regain myself—a fact, by the way, that certainly isn't true for every woman who experiences Powerful Mate Syndrome.

You see, in the world of powerful partners, even in these times of independent women, there remains an unspoken rule that wives are to put their mates' careers first and foremost in their lives. No, there is no official rulebook by which wives must abide, but there *is* an unspoken, subtle expectation that once you join the sorority of "Power Partners' Wives," your first priority should be to support him and his career. Everything else should take a back seat. Just think about what happens every time a man decides to declare himself a candidate for a political office; one of the first things people start speculating about is his wife. If she happens to be in the middle of performing brain surgery, she'd better finish that up pronto and get out there and campaign with that powerful partner of hers. You're supposed to attend every social event possible—looking like you just stepped out of *Vogue* magazine—make your home his castle, satiate his conjugal and culinary needs, and pretend as though you don't have anything that's as worthy of your attention as being the good little wife.

Of course I don't necessarily think that ending a marriage or a relationship is the answer for every woman who finds herself in this difficult situation, and James and I certainly had other issues that brought our marriage down. But had I approached the marriage more clear-eyed and with a strategy for success I would have been aware of the potential pitfalls inherent in a marriage to a powerful mate. At the time, though, there were no books, no therapists, and certainly no other wives I knew who were exploring what I have come to call Powerful Mate Syndrome. In fact, there existed a tacit understanding that "you just don't complain" about problems in your marriage, home, and family, especially when you seem to be living the fairy tale. Even in the face of public revelations of adultery, domestic violence, and reckless behavior, there is still a certain amount of stigma attached to the idea of refuting the existence of the fairy tale. Much like families with an alcoholic member, many women are apprehensive or ashamed about admitting that the very thing that they hoped for the most (to be married to a powerful mate) is bringing them so much pain, anxiety, and depression. But this is a problem that won't go away until we are willing to release our fantasies and get real about the bargain we are striking—and the challenges we face—when we marry "powerful" partners.

If you relate to my story or feel "lesser than" your powerful mate, no matter what kind of power you feel he possesses, I want you to ask yourself the following questions:

1. Do I like the person I am today? Do I know who that person staring back at me in the mirror really is?

2. Have I put my own personal and professional dreams and goals on hold?

3. Do I rely on my partner as the sole source of validation?

4. Do I fail to voice my opinions on matters that affect both of us?

5. Have I surrendered my interest in financial matters or allowed unqualified people assume control?

6. Have I turned to destructive, nonproductive habits to mask the pain of feeling out of control of my life?

7. Have I become complicit in creating my own invisibility?

8. Do I believe that I don't have the right to express my displeasure, disappointment, and disillusionment with my relationship?

9. Am I willing or able to fight for my right to have the career that would make me feel fulfilled?

10. Have I made my partner my "God" and made worshipping him my spiritual practice? (Really be honest with yourself on this one.)

If you answered yes to more than a few of the above, you may be suffering from Powerful Mate Syndrome as I was. Believe me, all is not lost. I, along with the many other women whose stories I will share in this book, have traveled through the dark, daunting tunnel that is Powerful Mate Syndrome, and we have emerged smarter, more confident, more fulfilled and mature women. I wrote this book to offer you a lifeline because this is the book that I wish had existed before I married my powerful prince. Had I known then what I know now, I'm sure that I still would have married James. After all, I was very much in love with him. But I would have had a much greater understanding of the forces and challenges that lay ahead. Most importantly, I would have known that despite what the outside world considers powerful, within my marriage I had a right to be just as powerful as he, and that being an equal participant in the relationship was not optional. It was a prerequisite, and a nonnegotiable one.

When my marriage ended, I went back to school and attained a Master's degree in Clinical Psychology. In my work as a registered marriage and family therapy intern, I have seen many other women with PMS, and I have certainly known dozens of women in my life who fit the definition, too. While most women have some sort of power imbalance in their relationships, PMS is marked by an imbalance of power in almost *every* area of the relationship. It is a condition that involves betraying *ourselves,* and that's where the healing has to happen too—within ourselves. Whether our relationships are fixable or not, when we rid ourselves of the rescue fantasy, we learn to tap into our innate power to author the stories and situations that both empower us and fulfill our needs.

My detractors will say that I am overanalyzing marriage, making it all too complicated, and taking the romance out it. I know from my own experience that this is not true. Rather, I am disseminating some hard-won knowledge. Knowledge is power, and you can never have too much of it.

If you are in a relationship with, considering marriage to, or are already married to a powerful person, don't go another day without reading this book. It will encourage you to think in a more realistic way about what it means (and doesn't mean) to be in the relationship, which will enable you to consciously create a partnership that is more fulfilling, rewarding, and joyful than anything you ever dreamed or hoped for. You may not believe me yet, but you have the power and the courage to give up the fantasy and create a brilliant *reality* tale, a story based in real life, not fairy tales, a story that reflects your truest passions, your authentic values and desires, your deepest integrity. Here's to creating that reality tale, complete with a happy ending that lasts the rest of your life.

PART ONE

THE POWERFUL MATE SYNDROME

DEFINING POWERFUL MATE SYNDROME

"I slept, and dreamed that life was Beauty. I woke, and found that life was Duty."
—ELLEN STURGIS HOOPER, nineteenth-century poet

POWERFUL MATES come in many shapes and sizes. Perhaps a working definition would help. Let's start with the word *powerful*. Its meaning is always in the mind of the beholder, isn't it? Just like so many other words in our vocabulary, the way we perceive power has everything to do with our experience and our environment. A partner who is powerful to you may not seem powerful to anyone else. For the purposes of this book, I use the term *powerful mate* to describe *any intimate partner who has the ability to exert significant influence, both positive and negative, over your life.*

Note that one of the most important words in that definition is significant. The only person who has to be aware of this "significant" influence is you. Some people are generally believed to be powerful—the CEO of a Fortune 500 company, the heir to a worldwide hotel empire, heads of state, entertainment moguls, best-selling authors. But what about the person who runs a homeless shelter and provides meals, counseling, and employment assistance to displaced people? Is he (or, yes, she) a powerful person? He may not seem so to you, but to his spouse, who is constantly told by people in the community how wonderful her spouse is and how lucky she is to be married to him, he's not only powerful, but his power might be making her feel pretty invisible. Even if he never lords his status over her, she can succumb to Powerful Mate Syndrome—or what I like to call "the other PMS"—by doing it to herself. The point is, there are no hard, fast criteria for determining who is or isn't powerful. It isn't my idea of a powerful mate, or your family's, or your best friend's that counts. Being under the spell of a powerful mate is all a matter of *your perception.*

My powerful mate was a star athlete. Yours may be a teacher, an emergency room doctor, a plant supervisor, a local mayor, or a car dealer. He may be simply the smartest or most charming or persuasive personality in whatever room he enters. Powerful Mate Syndrome knows no class, race, or religion—and not even gender. What we have in common is that *we experience our mates as more powerful than we are.*

This is key. We *experience* our mates as powerful. It is a matter of our *perception* and of how we *relate* to that power. My former husband did not cause me to "catch" or "come down with" Powerful Mate Syndrome. PMS is what I call a "syndrome of the self," meaning that it is the result not of forces outside of oneself but of something lurking within the psyche. Of course this is not to say that the actions of our partners play no role. If your spouse is physically abusive, unfaithful, addicted to a substance like alcohol or drugs, or mentally cruel, he must be held accountable for his behavior. But he or she is not *the problem*. The way you give over power to him or her is.

Okay, so how did we all get here?

The Origins of Powerful Mate Syndrome

Despite the many gains women have made in the past thirty years or so, we are still, practically from birth, indoctrinated with the idea that someday the "right" man will come into our lives and bring with him the keys to our emotional, sexual, economic, and even social fulfillment.

Decades ago, that dream of being saved by a prince might have actually had a chance of coming true. Women didn't have a lot of options for becoming powerful themselves, and marrying power was often their only viable option. But since World War II, when even relatively middle-class white women were driven into the workforce in droves, the Civil Rights Movement, which fought for equal access and opportunities for all people, and the Feminist Movement, which had women everywhere questioning the so-called "natural" roles of the two sexes, the nature of relationships between men and women have been forever changed. Once women began to consider an alternative to being swept away by a handsome prince, once they began to consider that it was possible and maybe even preferable to stand on their own two feet rather than deriving their worth through someone else, once what I call TCOY messages—Take Care Of Yourself—became a part of women's psyche, the seeds of internal conflict were sown.

Most women today have received both messages. We heard the fairy tales, watched the movies, read the romance novels, and even today make time each week to live vicariously through the parade of characters on reality shows that perpetuate the myth that women can be saved by a powerful prince. At the same time, we were told that we were supposed to take care of ourselves; that we were solely responsible for creating our own happiness. Thus, in our subconscious are two trains—two conflicting impulses—on the same track. Unless and until we find a successful resolution, there is bound to be a catastrophic collision as the two impulses vie for superiority and dominance within our psyches. Countless scenarios are possible, the most important of which we will explore in the coming chapters. The bottom line is, many, many women continue to experience the collision of these two impulses: On the one hand, we know that we should be independent and strong, but God, wouldn't life be perfect if our prince would just show up already?

How Powerful Mate Syndrome Takes Root

The two things that enable Powerful Mate Syndrome to thrive in the psyche of women are naiveté and the insistence on maintaining the fantasy. Make no mistake. You can be highly intelligent and still be naive. They are not mutually exclusive. In fact, one has very little to do with the other. When I met my former husband, I was a freshman in college, fully engaged in the rigors of an academically challenging curriculum. I also worked part-time as an office assistant in the university's International Center. I had plenty of what my parents called "book sense," but when it came to men and relationships, I was naive and inexperienced. My knowledge about men, relationships, and, most important, about myself was limited. And, as I would come to realize many years later, I was very much under the influence of the fantasy-based notion of the prince that I was destined to connect with someday. While I was not yet afflicted with Powerful Mate Syndrome at the beginning of my relationship with James, the powerful prince fantasy was there. PMS would not happen until after we were married, and then it would become a self-fulfilling prophesy. Something shifted radically once we were married; something was markedly different. That difference was one of the keys to my battle with PMS.

How My Fairy Tale Began

With the benefit of hindsight, I can see that I was the prototypical woman for PMS. James and I met at the University of North Carolina. I was a good student and a cheerleader, and James was my fantasy prince—a starter on the varsity basketball team, tall, dark, and handsome, and a big man on campus. I had always liked guys who stood out among a crowd without trying, who weren't flashy, loud, or braggadocios, and that's what he seemed to me to be. James was friendly to everyone; he didn't travel with an entourage as is so common with athletes, and his demeanor seemed to belie his youth. I think I was also starved for a relationship at that time. I had not had a steady boyfriend since the tenth grade when I got my young tender heart chewed up and spit out by my high school sweetheart. I hadn't even gone to either my junior or senior high school prom. After such an extended period of emotional isolation, I think I was ripe for the picking. There is a saying: "When the student is ready, the teacher will come." Here was my teacher. Little did I know then just how much there was for me to learn.

We made a perfect Cinderella couple. The first year of our courtship was filled with excitement. The highlight came when North Carolina won the NCAA basketball championship in New Orleans. James was named the MVP of the tournament, which fueled speculation that he would leave school to enter the NBA draft. Sure enough, the following summer he chose to follow his dream to play professional basketball.

With that decision, our romance went from cross-campus to cross-country. For three years we endured a long-distance relationship. Then one evening James proposed. I had traveled to Los Angeles to visit him for a weekend in November of 1983. He had a game the Friday night that I arrived. At that time the Lakers were playing at the Fabulous Forum. He had a great game that night and afterwards we went to T.G.I. Fridays in the Marina for our postgame eating ritual. We went there often. The atmosphere was lively, the food was good, and it was close to where he lived at the time. We ordered our food and drinks and began catching up. Somewhere along the way, the conversation turned to how difficult it was to be apart for such long periods of time. Before I knew it, James was down on one knee saying, "I think it's time we go shopping for a size six." Well, my shoe size was definitely not a size six so I knew he was talking about rings. Frankly, I had been hinting around for months about my ring size, but this took me totally by surprise. I was completely overwhelmed. But without a moment's hesitation, I said yes.

That night I began making mental notes about **THE WEDDING!** The wedding is an integral part of every fairy tale, isn't it? No longer guided by my rational mind, I was now on fairy-tale autopilot.

Like so many women, I never stopped to consider who and what it was that I was vowing to commit to for the rest of my life. I became obsessed with the wedding rather than the marriage. Just take a look at any newsstand and notice how many magazines are devoted to weddings rather than to marriage. Not only is the wedding industry huge, generating billions of dollars every year, but most of us equate the size of the wedding with the success of the marriage. Of course if we stopped to think about it, we'd realize how absurd that is. A wedding is an event, a finite event, while a marriage is a constantly evolving process with a life and rhythm all its own. But I digress.

The trouble with the fairy tale is that the prince has to have a princess—someone to play the counterpart to his character. He's strong; she's weak. He leads; she follows. He gives orders; she follows through. I didn't have the wisdom to know that by putting on the princess's gown I was unwittingly agreeing to become a subordinate in my own relationship. For all intents and purposes my vows might as well have read, "I, Angela, take you James, to be my superior.

I promise to support your dreams and goals. I will stand by you through good times and bad. I pledge to become as inconspicuous as possible, to suppress my dreams and goals, to look the other way when I see things that I don't agree with, and to keep up the appearance of 'happily ever after' until death us do part."

The Assumptions We Make

One of the most egregious mistakes so many women make on their way to the land of Powerful Mate Syndrome is not taking the time to ask and honestly answer some of the following questions—whether you're already married, still dating, or preparing to walk down the aisle together:

- Am I trying to secure my own power by marrying a powerful mate?

- Is it the man or the fantasy that I am in love with?

- How are we going to share power in this relationship?

- Does he really see me as an equal?

- Will he have more power in the relationship because he makes more money than me?

- Is being married compatible with my other goals in life?

- What are the deal breakers in this marriage?

- Do I want to be with this man or do I *need* to be with him?

- Am I holding him to an unattainable standard?

- Am I marrying him in order to please someone other than myself?

- Am I trying to prove something other than my love for him by getting married?

The pull on us to have the fairy-tale relationship is so great that we resist using our good sense and reason. It is as if we believe fairies will encircle our relationship with a magical coat of armor that is impervious to the pressures and problems that exert themselves on all of us. If we could put our questions, concerns, and quibbles about our relationship down on paper, we might begin to break the hold that fantasy and naiveté have on us. We would also begin to form the basis of a relationship grounded in reality instead of trying to live up to a nonexistent fantasy.

Ask anyone who has a happy and fulfilling relationship and they will tell you, if they are truthful, that it is anything but a fairy tale. The most successful relationships are reality tales, not fairy tales, and they are written by the people in them, not by some author with a vivid imagination.

My story is not unique, of course. It parallels that of many women. Take for example the story of Ginger and Mark.* Ginger was an accomplished artist and sculptor with a small but loyal following. For five years she dated Mark, a talented

*These are pseudonyms.

cartoonist with a daily syndicated comic strip. Theirs was a happy courtship filled with lectures at the local university, Ginger's art shows, travel to foreign countries, and their mutual love of collecting rare cookie jars. Ginger assumed that their marriage would be a continuation of the fun and carefree times that they had shared during their courtship. Initially they were going to elope, but the pressure from family members, especially Ginger's three sisters, became so great that they chose a traditional wedding at a ritzy local hotel instead. It was a beautiful affair but it cost nearly ten thousand dollars more than Ginger and Mark had set aside for the wedding. Their plans to buy a new home had to be postponed until they paid off their wedding debts.

They had never talked about having children, since they both were in their forties, but in the second year of their marriage Ginger became pregnant with their son. Mark Jr. was born later that year. Since Mark worked from home in a small office above their garage, Ginger assumed that he would become "Mr. Mom," the baby's primary caregiver, after the baby was weaned. That would enable her to go back to work in her studio which was located nearly twenty miles from their home. It was a space that she had rented jointly with two other artists since long before Mark came into her life.

Mark assumed that Ginger would put her career on hold indefinitely or at least until they found a good day care center for Mark Jr. Ginger was vehemently opposed to putting the baby in day care until he was at least four years old. Mark believed that because he was the major breadwinner he should not have to change his schedule. His earnings were enough to take care of the family. Anyway, he reasoned, if his mother had stayed home to raise him and his siblings, then Ginger could take some time off from her career to raise Mark Jr. What Mark failed to grasp, even with his vast intellectual prowess, was that Ginger was cut from different cloth than his mother. What Ginger failed to realize was that her lack of communication about her intent to continue her career after the baby was born would come back to haunt her.

Ginger believed that Mark was the power broker in their relationship and reluctantly gave up her interest in the art studio. She stopped creating artwork and became a full-time stay-at-home mom with Mark Jr. No longer was her identity derived from the work that she loved. The thing that had contributed so greatly to her self-esteem disappeared. Now she was Mark's wife and Mark Jr.'s mother. Mark became her primary source of validation. Her growth and self-development sputtered. She was now a two-dimensional figure rather than a three-dimensional one. Ginger had a classic case of PMS.

Let me make it clear once again that I am not asserting that there is anything wrong or less than honorable about being a stay-at-home mom. I was one myself and I have many friends whom I respect and admire that choose to stay at home and care for their children. I think that the job of staying home with young children is often much more challenging than going to a nine-to-five job. Nevertheless, I believe that a woman should base her decision on the reality of her situation rather than some fantasy that being at home will be like *Leave it to Beaver* or *The Donna Reed*

Show. Ginger gave up her work not because she thought it was the best thing for the baby or her family but because she believed that Mark's wishes carried more weight than her own. She believed he had more power in the relationship than she.

Ginger and Mark's story illustrates the fact that regardless of who you are marrying or how effectively you can convince yourself that your relationship is perfect, you both need to be clear about your goals, expectations, and limitations.

Some people will bristle at the suggestion of conducting structured discussions about a relationship and the people in it. Some will say that it takes the romance out of the relationship. I disagree completely. It may sound like a paradox, but I believe that the more clear and concrete the framework you build around your relationship, the more you approach it as reality and not fantasy, the greater the space you will create within it for both you and your partner to reach your potential as individuals and partners.

I had hoped for a marriage that would last a lifetime. I had hoped to have four children. I had hoped to raise my children in a home where they had both parents present at all times. I had hoped for a fairy tale. Hoping didn't make any of those things come true. There is a tremendous difference between hoping for something and being willing to do the work that is necessary to bring your desires to fruition. Hoping keeps you in the fog of naiveté and fantasy. Working—yes, working—puts you in the realm of possibility and reality. Why couldn't I abandon the fantasy? There were several reasons. First, like so many other first-time brides, I didn't want to believe that anything about marriage included work. Marriage is supposed to be carefree and easy; it's supposed to flow along with no rough spots, right? Wrong! But that isn't what we tell ourselves. We lie to ourselves to avoid the discomfort that might arise if we really probed our deepest thoughts about marriage, our intended spouse, and ourselves. It can be very scary territory.

Your thoughts about marriage are like unexplored forestland on the path leading to a satisfying marriage. You cannot go around the forest. There may be all kinds of scary creatures lurking in there that you don't want to deal with. However, not going into the forest is not going to make the creatures disappear. They'll just wait until you get enough willpower to venture in. What happens when you encounter them is your decision. You can either confront them or you can run away from them. If you deal with them immediately you have a choice as to whether you want to press on with your journey or turn back. However, if you choose not to deal with them at all, you simply end up stuck in the same spot. Eventually you will be forced to deal with the creatures either in this relationship or another one. Only you can slay the creatures.

When I married James, I thought I knew everything there was to know about marriage. No one could tell me anything. I was smug, arrogant, and ignorant. That's one of the things that comes along with marrying someone with money: You begin to believe that having money exempts you from the problems other people have to struggle with. And other people fall prey to the fantasy, too, buying into the illusion that the "perfect couple" is above the challenges everyone else faces. (You only have to look at all the millionaires who end up in divorce court every year to know this is untrue.) The same fantasy takes hold with other forms of outward success and power too—with the same unfortunate results.

Were there warning signs that indicated that James and I might have problems in our relationship? Of course there were. Did I acknowledge them and sit down and discuss them with him? Of course I did not. That would have forced me to admit that I wasn't living a fairy tale. I didn't know then that the chances of my marriage surviving would have been exponentially improved had I done so. And even if it had still ended, I would have had far better tools for getting back onto my own two feet.

The Symptoms of Powerful Mate Syndrome

On the face of it, Powerful Mate Syndrome might sound like just a clever new package for other psychological issues such as depression, anxiety, or an old-fashioned inferiority complex, but I have seen too many women experience the befuddlement and anguish that comes from losing their identity to a powerful mate to ignore the signs. This syndrome has its own unique patterns. Its sufferers may not be clinically depressed, they may not have acute anxiety, but they are dying inside. As I see it, there are two factors that distinguish Powerful Mate Syndrome from these other psychological problems: the presence of a powerful partner, and the belief or perception that one's mate is more powerful than one is. (Whether or not the belief is true is irrelevant. It is the mere existence of the belief that matters.)

Bear in mind that this is a "syndrome of the self." Like anorexia, where the patient's *belief* that she is overweight controls her behavior, with PMS it is the *belief* in the idea that her mate is more powerful that controls her, not the idea itself.

With those two critical factors present, a woman with Powerful Mate Syndrome:

- experiences a profound loss of identity

- subjugates or abandons her own dreams and goals in favor of those of her mate

- excessively relies on her mate as the sole or primary source of self-esteem, validation, and feelings of well-being

- neglects her own self-care, growth, and development

These four fundamental characteristics form the basis of Powerful Mate Syndrome. All of us can probably think of someone who exhibits all or most of them. They describe my married self completely. If you think you may be suffering from Powerful Mate Syndrome but aren't sure, turn the page and take the PMS Quiz. You do not have to share your findings with anyone else, so be brutally honest with your answers.

TAKE THE PMS QUIZ

Assign one point for each statement that resonates with you.
Assign a zero for each statement that does not resonate with you.
Refer to the scale at the end of the quiz.

To what degree do these statements resonate with you?	Does resonate with me (1 point)	Does not resonate (0 points)
1. It isn't important for me to have my own source of income if my husband earns a good living.		
2. I often feel like an appendage of my mate rather than my own person.		
3. I am willing to sacrifice myself if it is necessary to keep my family and home intact.		
4. I am a different person when I am around my mate than when I'm not.		
5. I have not lived up to my potential in many areas of my life.		
6. It is important to me not to overshadow my mate's accomplishments.		
7. My mate's public image is more important to me than my self-image.		
8. I felt as though I had more influence over the direction my life took *before* I got married.		
9. I will not pursue my goals unless I have my mate's blessing.		
10. I don't feel entitled to work because my mate's income has made us financially secure.		
11. I often wonder what happened to the person I used to be.		

12. I would rather be in an "emotionally bankrupt" relationship with my powerful mate than risk being alone.		
13. I have done things that are immoral or illegal in order to protect my mate's image.		
14. I am a "silent partner" in my relationship.		
15. I care about what my friends would think if I decided to end my marriage.		
16. My mate is man enough to satisfy my every need.		
17. It is difficult to be with my mate without taking a drink or using some type of drugs.		
18. Sex is the currency I use to get what I want from my mate.		
19. Without my mate, I would be nobody.		
20. I am not worthy of having everything I want in my life because I already have so much.		
21. I married a powerful mate because of the status and wealth that go along with the marriage.		
22. I am unable to effectively communicate my needs to my mate.		
23. Having my mate's approval is of the utmost importance to me.		
24. I don't like the person I have become.		
25. My life is full of material things and other outward signs of success but I feel like something is missing.		
26. I don't share my vulnerabilities with my mate because I don't want to appear to be dependent.		

27. I know how to take care of everyone's needs except my own.		
28. If my mate died suddenly, I would not know how to handle my financial matters.		
29. As long as I look good on the outside, it doesn't matter that I feel so bad on the inside.		
30. Rather than risk a disagreement, my mate and I talk about everything except our relationship.		
Total Score		

SCORING

If your score is **20 or more points:** You have either already succumbed to PMS or are at high risk for doing so. You have given the responsibility for your life to your mate. You need to reassess your goals and reconnect with yourself. Your life and relationship need a major overhaul. You have much work to do, but it can certainly be done. Read on.

If your score is **19 to 11 points:** You have a strong propensity to succumb to PMS but you haven't fallen into the abyss yet. Your sense of self-worth and identity could be strengthened. Your relationship could use a tune-up. It's time to take stock of your goals for your life and your relationship. You have some work to do. Read on.

If your score is **10 points or less:** You may have a few issues but you've still got the upper hand on PMS. On the pages that follow you'll learn how you can prevent it from taking hold in your relationship. You have the opportunity to be proactive and create the relationship you want. Read on.

What PMS Is Not

Before we move on, let's take a look at what Powerful Mate Syndrome is *not. It is not:*

- Race, age, or gender specific, although it does dispropor- tionately affect women.

- Related to premenstrual syndrome, menstruation, or menopause.

- Clinical depression. Powerful Mate Syndrome may be ac- companied by depression, in which case it should be treated by a licensed mental health practitioner or a physician.

- Postpartum depression. Anyone who suspects they have postpartum depression should seek care from a licensed mental health practitioner or a physician.

- Powerful Mate Syndrome is not a disorder included in the Diagnostic and Statistical Manual of Mental Disorders published by the American Psychiatric Association.

- Based on socio-economic status.

- Life-threatening, although it greatly diminishes the qual- ity of one's life experiences and primary relationships.

If you believe that you have succumbed to Powerful Mate Syndrome or are on the way to doing so, read on. For some people, it may be the desire to understand what took place in a prior relationship where PMS was in effect that warrants delving deeper into this book. Whether your concern is about a past, present, or possible future relationship, you have already taken one of the most important steps in either reclaiming or maintaining your strength and purpose by acknowledging that you've got some work to do. Many women, including myself, have overcome Powerful Mate Syndrome, and you can, too. This is not about leaving your marriage, blaming either your partner or yourself for the travails that have befallen you, or making excuses. This is about owning your power as it pertains to you as an individual and as a partner to your "powerful" mate. Remember: Your powerful mate is not your adversary; the surrendering of your own strength and sense of self is. When you begin to see the distinction between the two, you will begin to empower yourself to create a life, and perhaps a relationship far more fulfilling than any fairy tale could ever be.

As changes begin to occur in your thoughts and actions, there cannot help but be changes in your relationship. Initially such changes may be met with suspicion or resistance from your partner. Change is often a scary thing and you need to acknowledge your partner's feelings without judgment or criticism. John Bradshaw says, "A family or relationship is like a mobile. You can't move one piece without causing movement in the other ones." One positive way of looking at your partner's response is as a sign that she or he is attuned to whatever is taking place in your life. Whatever affects you most likely affects your partner. The absence of a reaction, either negative or positive, would be of greater concern to me than a bit of fear of change. The payoff for working through the fear is well worth the effort.

In the coming chapter we will examine different types of powerful mates and what it is about them that triggers the "Powerful Prince" fantasy within us. You may begin to see your mate in a whole new way and, in turn, you may begin to understand some of the decisions and actions you have taken in response to the person you have perceived him to be.

What type of powerful mate did you choose to cocreate your reality tale? What was it about him that made him attractive to you? Did you fall in love with the person or the image, his character or charisma, or was it his brains or his brawn? It's possible that it was all or none of those things. You might have chosen the person who came closest to your idea of "The Prince" without regard to who he really was. Curious? Read on.

2

SIX TYPES OF POWERFUL MATES

**"It were all one that I should love a particular star,
And think to wed it, he is so above me."**
—WILLIAM SHAKESPEARE, *Twelfth Night*

PEOPLE ACQUIRE power in many ways. Some are born into power by virtue of their family name—be it Rockefeller or Kennedy or Carnegie or DuPont. Others gain it through professional or career success. Still others take it from others by force. Pioneers, inventors, innovators, and entrepreneurs create their own power by tapping into niches that no one else has. And then there are those who believe they can acquire power by association, in our case, marriage.

There is no stronger aphrodisiac in the world than power. What is the one thing that can make an old man with one foot in the grave and the other on a banana peel a much-sought-after catch, and a potbellied, balding head of a movie studio attractive to a beautiful and ambitious young woman? The answer is power. Why does a secretary have an affair with her boss? Why does a college student become enamored with her professor? Sure, there may be other factors, but the element of power is present in each of these scenarios. In fact, power can mask a multitude of otherwise objectionable or even offensive characteristics. Sometimes the prospect of attaining power through marriage leads women to compromise their values and barter with their bodies.

Living in Los Angeles, I see ample evidence of this. A lunchtime visit to any upscale restaurant illustrates the point. At table after table you will find young Hollywood wannabes partnered with suitors old enough to be their grandfathers. They are busy crafting their fairy tales. There's just one thing that most of these ambitious young women don't realize. You can't marry power! You can marry into a powerful family or you can marry someone who is powerful in a certain niche, but his power is *his*. You don't magically become powerful yourself just because you exchange wedding vows with a powerful person. Without a doubt, Princess Diana was the most poignant example of this. She literally married her prince and hoped to have a fairy-tale marriage. When the fantasy crashed and the marriage ended, she began to write her own reality tale, but sadly she died before she could fully enjoy her newfound power and happiness.

Let's look at the different kinds of powerful mates through whom so many women hope to live their fairy tale.

The Wealthy Mate

This is an easy one. From childhood, we are all told the same bull: Wealth brings happiness. A wealthy mate is considered an obvious "great catch." Especially for women from less privileged circumstances, wealthy men seem to be the ticket to paradise. Parents, who often pin hopes for a better life on their daughters' choice of a mate, can get hooked by the idea that a prince will come to take their daughter away to live a fairy-tale life "happily ever after." Of course, daughters themselves get hooked by this fantasy too—and sometimes get what they wish for.

Let's be honest here. Seduction by dollar signs often outweighs concerns about character. Just think about it. Which potential son-in-law do you think is more likely to get a parents' blessing: John, the son of the founder and owner of the local country club or Jack, the son of the manager of the local convenience store? Even if everyone agrees that Jack is the nicer guy, John usually wins the contest hands down.

Of course, you don't have to be famous to be wealthy. Do you know the name of the millionaire who manufactures dry cleaning bags? Retro athletic jerseys? In fact, a great deal of the monetary wealth in this world is possessed by people you and I have never heard of.

Lucas M. is not famous but he is wealthy. He grew up in a middle-class family in the suburbs of Chicago and always dreamed of being an optometrist. He also had an interest in men's fashion. While attending college, Lucas worked part-time in an optical shop. It was there that he began to think about the possibility of owning his own optical shop where he could sell his own designer eyeglass frames. He opened his first optical shop two years after he graduated from college with money that he had saved and several small loans from friends. Now he has five shops in Chicago, three in Los Angeles, one in South Beach, and two in New York City. His stores generate enough income for him and his wife, Amelia, to have homes in Chicago and Los Angeles, a summer home in the Hamptons, and a beachside condominium on the Hawaiian island of Kauai.

If Lucas were to walk into a room of a hundred people all wearing glasses, it is possible that no one would recognize him. But it is highly probable that at least fifty of those people would be wearing a pair of his high-fashion eyeglass frames. That translates into wealth—and power. The fact that Lucas is a "capital-creating machine" gives him the power and connections to make things happen. He can pick up his telephone and within minutes get commitments from heads of major retail operations, photographers, entertainers, and others with whom he has a relationship, to do things that a person without his wealth could not.

Amelia and Lucas were introduced to each other by Lucas's design partner, Richard, and his wife, Bethany. Richard, Bethany, and Amelia had become friends while attending design school together. Richard and Bethany believed that Lucas and Amelia would make a well-suited couple in light of their common interest in design and the arts. They arranged an evening of dinner and drinks at a local jazz club. Their hunch was right. Lucas and Amelia had strong chemistry from the first hello. After a yearlong courtship, Lucas asked for Amelia's hand in marriage. In Amelia's mind she had met her prince. Why wouldn't she marry Lucas? He was handsome and charismatic. He had a lucrative business of his own and he would be an invaluable asset to her own textile design business. His social circle was filled with wealthy and exciting people. He could give her the kind of life most young women dream about. In short, he made her feel like a princess. Six months later, they married in a lovely ceremony, paid for entirely by Lucas and hosted by Richard and Bethany at their home.

When they married, Lucas was already wealthy and established. Amelia had managed to make a decent living, but she wasn't enjoying the same level of success as Lucas. She had launched a line of women's hand-painted T-shirts and handbags. There was a lot of competition, but she was determined to break through and somehow distinguish her products from her competitors'. After she and Lucas got married, she brought her line under the umbrella of Lucas's products. They kept her name on the bags and shirts but displayed and sold them in his stores. That helped to boost interest in her products in the short run, but it was a short-lived turnaround. As the sales of her products slumped, so too did Amelia's spirits. She began to compare the amount of money Lucas was making to the amount she was. Of course there was no comparison. She neither produced the same income nor did her product line have the same name recognition. Perhaps ironically, none of this mattered to Lucas, but it mattered a great deal to Amelia. He knew how difficult it was to make a go of it in retail and he was there to support Amelia in every way that he could.

Amelia, rather than going back to the drawing board and devising a new strategy for her business, began to feel as though she shouldn't work as hard as she had been because Lucas was making enough to provide them with a lavish lifestyle. Instead of working five days a week as she had done previously, she cut her work week to three days. On her two free days a week, she either lunched with her girlfriends or spent the day shopping. The first year of that was fun. There were always plenty of girlfriends around to lunch with and she even started taking in the occasional movie or play when Lucas worked late, which he often did. His business continued to expand. The only things of hers that were expanding were her dress size and the number of unopened shoe boxes and garment bags in her closet.

Eventually Amelia decided to close her business altogether and live off the income Lucas's boutiques generated. By now her products had become an afterthought in the minds of most people because she failed to update and market them. She loved designing, but the rigors of business proved to be more challenging than she had ever anticipated. She decided she could "draft" off the success of Lucas's empire. Drafting, a term used in cycling, is when one cyclist intentionally gets behind another in order to avoid the slowing effect of the headwinds that the rider in front experiences. It decreases the amount of resistance and therefore results in a positive benefit. But she was wrong. She mistook her fatigue from fighting the retail wars for no longer needing something that would give her a sense of self. She ran up the white flag—not only on her business but also, unwittingly, on herself.

Amelia began to feel jealous of Lucas's success in business. The admiration that she once felt for him had now transformed into envy of the satisfaction that he derived from his work. The time and energy he had spent trying to help her grow her business he now put into his own. Their mutual love of design and growing their small businesses had been something they had in common. Now, with Amelia's business closed, this was no longer a source of closeness and shared purpose. To her acquaintances and even her friends, Amelia was now known solely as "the wife of Lucas M.," not as a designer and businesswoman in her own right. She didn't feel much like a princess anymore. In fact, she began to feel very poorly about herself. Although money was really never an issue in matters of her own health and wellness, Amelia stopped working out with her trainer because she had always used her own money to pay for it. Now that she was relying on Lucas for all of her money, she didn't feel entitled to keep the personal trainer. With the departure of the trainer came the arrival of the uncontrolled weight gain. With the weight gain came depression. Amelia was in a downward spiral.

Over time Amelia experienced a profound loss of identity. She went from a budding designer with her own business to simply the wife of a wealthy man. He did not force her to give up her business, which was her primary source of validation and self-esteem. In fact, he did the opposite, trying to mentor and encourage her. When the demands of his business increased, he was less and less able to provide her with validation or to try to buoy her feelings of well-being. She began to neglect her own self-care. She stifled her growth both as a businesswoman and as a wife. She attempted to fill the holes in her spirit with material things and food. Amelia is the poster woman for so many women who are married to wealthy, powerful mates and who succumb to Powerful Mate Syndrome. Are you one of them? If so, don't despair, you can redirect your life in a more positive direction. Read on.

The Famous Mate

Our culture's obsession with fame may be even greater than it is with wealth. Fame is often seen as the ultimate form of power. In ways that simply having money cannot, fame can grant a person access, influence, respect, and attention. Many people from wealthy families get married every year, but even those from the highest rung of society don't get the kind of attention that Jessica Simpson and Nick Lachey have gotten. Why don't we care about those other folks? Because they are not famous. They're wealthy, but that only gets you so much mileage. I know for a fact that if I had married one of my high school boyfriends, even if he had been financially successful, there would not have been seven hundred and fifty people at my wedding, there would have been no need to hire private security, and I certainly would not have been the subject of an extensive story in the newspaper the following Sunday. Our wedding would have gotten the same standard two-paragraph write-up that everyone else's did.

Famous princes actually have a particular burden. They're walking targets in a giant game of "Pin the Tail on the Donkey." Only it isn't a tail that women are trying to pin on him, it's the happily-ever-after fairy tale and the mantle of the rescuing prince, regardless of whether he wants or deserves it. The famous powerful mate is more likely to have greater expectations thrust upon him than any of the other types because of all the hoopla surrounding him. If he's famous, we feel as though we already know him. He has already taken on modern mythic qualities and we begin to create assumptions based on nothing but material that has been carefully crafted by clever public relations firms or media outlets. We assume that because he is a phenomenal quarterback or platinum-selling recording artist or charismatic public speaker or an Academy Award–winning actor or from a well-known political family, he will be a great husband. And the delusions go on and on. We simply assume that because a man is famous he's a prince. It's no wonder so many of us end up disillusioned, disappointed, and divorced. Actions based on faulty assumptions produce faulty results.

Being in a relationship with a famous, powerful mate can be a catch-22. On the one hand, he may be able to provide you with opportunities that you wouldn't otherwise have (or at least you wouldn't have them as quickly or easily without him). If you're a budding actress and you want to get in to meet with the top brass of some of the major studios, having a relationship with an A-list actor might be your ticket in. If you are an aspiring singer and you want to get your demo into the hands of a major record-label head, having a relationship with a multiplatinum-selling artist would probably get you access that you wouldn't otherwise have. If you think that sounds cynical or sexist, think again. Those of us who have chosen to see life the way it really is know that people enter into relationships all the time with the intention of furthering their own agendas rather than for love or companionship. What many of them don't realize is that for every potential positive to being in such a relationship, there is usually a commensurate negative. Sometimes a woman wants the fairy tale—whether the fairy-tale relationship or the fairy-tale career—so badly that she is willing to suppress or deny all evidence that doesn't jibe with her fantasy.

Trisha was one of those women, and Chase her famous, powerful prince. Chase is a famous and wealthy musician. In addition to his own solo singing career, he produces and writes music for artists in rock, hip-hop, and country music. He has been around the music industry for some time, but he is still very much in touch with the current trends. Trisha is also a singer. She has worked as a background vocalist for numerous music artists as well as appeared in several music videos. Her dream was to make the jump from background artist to major headliner. Even though he was married, in Trisha's mind Chase was "the prince" long before she ever met him. She was fortunate to work with him on a video shoot, and at the wrap party she slipped a copy of her demo tape into his pocket. He took it home and listened to it. He was quite impressed with what he heard and called her to arrange lunch the following week.

Chase agreed to take Trisha on as a development project. They began writing songs together, working in the studio long hours, and spending more and more time with one another. Before either of them realized it, their working relationship had turned into a romantic one, with clandestine weekends spent in luxurious hotels and resorts. A chance encounter with a photographer from a weekly celebrity magazine blew the cover off their affair. For Chase's wife, this latest revelation was the straw that broke the camel's back. She retained the best divorce attorney she could find and, in the least amount of time allowed under the law, she and Chase were divorced. Trisha hated that Chase had to go through the divorce, but the flip side of it was that the publicity was great for her career. Chase and Trisha married only four months after his divorce was final.

At first, being married to Chase seemed like a fairy tale to Trisha. He was protective and nurturing, and he guided her through many of the career hurdles she faced. Her career took off like a rocket with a CD that went platinum and multiple television appearances on the late-night talk show circuit. Chase's nurturing began to encompass everything that had to do with Trisha, including who she associated with, the songs she would sing on her next CD, the clothes she wore, the venues that she played, and the publications to which she gave interviews. Because he had such a successful track record both as an artist and a producer, Trisha believed that she did not have a leg to stand on when she tried to challenge his decisions. She felt smothered. It seemed to her that she was a prisoner in her fairy tale rather than a princess. Because Chase was so powerful in the music industry, Trisha resigned herself to doing things his way, yet deep down inside she felt that she had a better understanding of how to best utilize her talent. Underneath the calm, successful exterior was a sad, disillusioned princess who had gotten exactly what she wished for: a famous, powerful mate.

Trisha's career continued to flourish. She sold millions and millions of CDs, but true happiness eluded her. Why? Because she had become Chase's creation. A product of his engineering, not of her desires and dreams for herself. She might as well have been one of the Stepford Wives. To the public she had a definite identity and image, but to herself, her identity was lost. Chase became the filter through which all information and ideas flowed. If it was approved or validated by Chase, then it was good. Trisha leaned on him as the source of her feelings of self-worth and well-being. What she got was an increase in her net worth, not her self-worth.

She turned her growth and development over to Chase. Not only had he become her husband, he was her handler, her guru, her mind and soul. She was everything with him and nothing without him. At least that was what she began to believe.

Never had she imagined that Chase, her ticket to stardom and a happy life, would also be her ticket to becoming invisible to everyone except her adoring fans, even herself. Executives in the industry saw her as Chase's wife. Other performers saw her as Chase's creation. And other women regarded her as Chase's appendage. What Trisha thought would be a win-win situation was in actuality a win-lose situation. She won a mate. She won a career. But in the bargain she lost herself. She went into the marriage with her eyes wide open but ultimately found herself with Powerful Mate Syndrome.

Trisha could have allowed Chase to guide her career without handing over complete control of her life to him *if* she had been able to discern the difference between the two. It is altogether possible to be in a relationship with a powerful, successful, and famous man like Chase without becoming his appendage and a PMS sufferer. But it requires the woman to see her mate *as a man*, not a fairy-tale prince endowed with extraordinary powers, expertise about everything in life, and the ability to make her into a fairy-tale princess. Furthermore, it requires that the woman know where she ends and her husband begins. Even in marriage we remain separate people—ideally with common goals, but separate people nevertheless. It's somewhat like riding a tandem bicycle. You've both got to pedal or you're not going to get to your intended destination.

In fact, being in a relationship with a famous, powerful mate can be a wonderfully exciting experience *as long as you are able to see your mate and your relationship through the lens of reality, not rose-colored glasses.* In Chase and Trisha's case, Chase was just being who and what he had always been. It was up to Trisha to first wake up from the fairy tale that she was living in and, second, find the wherewithal to declare her goals and dreams for herself. Princes, no matter how wonderful, can't instinctively know our needs and desires. That is just more fairy-tale thinking. Trisha and Chase ended both their marriage and their musical collaboration. After assessing what had happened in his relationship with Trisha, Chase decided to mend his relationship with his former wife. They are now dating each other exclusively. Chase continues to write and record music of his own. He also continues to produce other artists' projects. Trisha never worked with Chase again. In fact, their relationship ended with her publicly declaring him somewhat of a Svengali. She branched out and sought the help of various producers and lyricists. Her career continues to soar. In the realm of relationships, Trisha has decided that she should not rush into a serious relationship until she is a bit more settled. In the meantime, she is casually dating several people.

The mythology that surrounds dating a famous person will never die. It lives on in our fantasy-infested minds and will continue to do so as long as there are famous people. We are seduced by it just as Snow White was seduced to bite the perfect red apple that she was offered by the nasty witch. We want to bite those apples, but we have no idea what biting them might bring.

The Mate Who Is Prominent in the Community

There are prominent and powerful people in every community, whether there are one hundred or one hundred thousand residents. They are not necessarily handsome, not necessarily famous outside their own milieu, but their prominence in their communities makes them powerful mate material. A mayor of a small town would certainly be powerful mate material, even if no one outside the county had ever heard of him, as would the president of a community college. You don't necessarily have to admire what they do or understand it, but you do have to acknowledge that whatever it is it provides value to someone. If you are the head football coach in a small town in Texas where high school football is looked upon as an almost religious experience, then you are definitely a prominent person in your community.

Then, of course, there is prominence that is based on the size of your business rather than contribution to your community. If you live in Wisconsin and your mate, Cranford, owns and runs the largest dairy farm in your community, he is surely a prominent person amongst the dairy farmers. That he possesses considerable wealth is most likely a given, but what's important here is that he has influence. His words and his actions are likely to have as much value in the community as his net worth. If he stands up in a convention of cattle owners in the state and declares that he has found a new kind of feed that he believes is better for his herd and his production capabilities, chances are great that others are going to follow suit. Any old John Doe would not have the power to influence the masses as this dairy farmer does. Cranford leads; they follow.

But then there is the Cranford that you see at home. He believes in marriage being the way it used to be in the "good ol' days." At the end of the day, he sits in front of the television watching the twenty-four-hour Farm Network, rarely helps with the household chores (that's woman's work), and seldom inquires about your day. Yet, you're there with the meatloaf, mashed potatoes, and peas ready for dinner, the house is spotless, and everything is in order. He's no leader in your household, yet when he says jump, you say, "How high?" Why? Because you've decided that if Cranford's word is good enough for the entire cattlemen's association to follow, then you'll follow it at home. You've become just as passive as the cows that he owns out in the pasture. Let me share with you again something that my daddy once told me: "The view never changes unless you're the lead cow."

The High-Achieving Professional Mate

Then there are the high achievers. These are men who often could not have gained their status and stature without some great sacrifices on the part of their wives.

Sandra helped Steven achieve great success in his career, and the price was Powerful Mate Syndrome. The very success that she helped him bring into fruition is, to her, "proof" that he is more powerful in the relationship than she. Clearly this is only her perception, not reality. She has adopted society's criteria by taking his public success and all it entails and imposing it on the relationship. She aided him in creating a successful business but neglected her own professional goals, convincing herself that her goals were not as worthy as his. After all, the princess is supposed to do whatever she can to support the prince, right? The trouble was, she could not support him without seeing herself as operating at a deficit.

Sandra grew up in suburban New Jersey. Around the age of fourteen she began to take an interest in the decorating publications that her mother subscribed to such as *Architectural Digest* and *Better Homes and Gardens*. When she graduated from high school she knew that one day she wanted to create beautiful interiors for people's homes and offices. She was fascinated by furniture, fabrics, and the latest design trends. She attended Pratt Institute School of Art and Design in New York City.

After graduation, Sandra returned home to live with her parents while she devised her strategy for getting work as an interior designer and eventually becoming the owner of her own firm. She did not intend to live the rest of her life in her hometown. A few weeks after settling into her parent's home, Sandra received a call from Betsy, an old friend from high school.

Betsy had an interest in the domestic arts and drew her inspiration from women like B. Smith and Martha Stewart. For two years she took every cooking, catering, and home-decorating course she could find at the local community college. Then she opened her own catering business with a small loan from her parents. It proved to be both challenging and rewarding in many ways.

Betsy also had a lot going on in her personal life. She was engaged to Kirk, who worked for the city as a mechanical engineer. Betsy and Kirk were hosting a small dinner party for a few of their friends and wanted to invite Sandra. Although they didn't tell her, the party was actually a Tupperware party, and the salesperson was a close male friend of theirs to whom they wanted to introduce Sandra. She gladly accepted their invitation.

The night of Betsy and Kirk's party arrived. Sandra was one of ten guests. Some were couples but most of them were singles like her. And then there was Steven—"Mr. Tupperware." His show was the first part of the evening. None of the other guests knew what was in store for them, but it was an evening they would never forget.

Steven's show was broken into four acts, complete with music and costume changes. It was absolutely incredible. Sandra, as well as all the other guests, was left speechless. What was even more amazing to her was that he did it all without ever appearing to be effeminate. On the contrary, he was able to be very sensual and very masculine at the same time. The men found the show to be just as entertaining as the women. And most important, Steven sold thousands of dollars worth of Tupperware that night and secured three commitments for future parties on the spot.

Betsy, the consummate party planner, served hors d'oeuvres, while Steven changed out of his costume. Sandra was giddy with the anticipation of getting to know him better. After all, he was one of the singles Betsy and Kirk had invited to the party.

As soon as he joined everyone, Kirk introduced Sandra and Steven. He was taller and more attractive than she had initially noted. She was nervous at first, but after a few minutes of conversation facilitated by Kirk, her anxiety was replaced by a feeling of ease. It almost felt like being with an old friend. Betsy had cleverly planned the seating arrangement at dinner so that they sat next to each other. That dinner party was the first night of what would eventually evolve into a whirlwind romance and a wedding one year later.

During their courtship, Sandra would accompany Steven to as many of his Tupperware party/shows as she could. Each night was different; Steven had a real knack for improvisation depending on who his audience was. She was continually impressed with the way both men and women embraced him. It seemed as though he was doing more than selling a product; he was providing a service. Many times people who came to the party with no intention of buying anything left with orders for hundreds of dollars worth of Tupperware products.

In fact, the demand for his parties began to exceed his availability, so he began to train other people to produce parties in the way that he did. Very rapidly, Steven managed to parlay what began as a way to earn some extra pocket money into a business valued into the high six-figures.

Sandra studied Steven's ability to market himself and his product with the intention of applying what she learned to her interior design pursuits. But she had become so involved in his business that she didn't give hers equal attention. She still loved design and longed to break away from being his "stagehand" to pursue her own interests. But the pull he had on her was like a magnetic energy field. When she knew she should be putting her energy into finding clients, she was out searching secondhand shops and costume stores with him.

She began to handle booking the parties and coordinating the delivery of the products to customers, relegating her commitment to the design business to what little bit she could fit in between Steven's gigs. It didn't help her either that he constantly told her how much he loved being able to share the business with her. It only deepened the conflict she felt about supporting him while at the same time feeling the need to pursue her own separate interests. She loved helping him and yet she pined for something of her own: something that would elicit validation and praise from other people as a result of her own efforts rather than his.

Sandra was suffering. She had gotten an innovative, creative, hardworking husband in the deal but had become a shadow of her former self. That is one of the insidious things that happens to a person who becomes afflicted with Powerful Mate Syndrome. She unwittingly displaces her own goals with those of her powerful mate and channels energies that she should expend on her own activities into her mate's because she believes that her mate's goals are more worthwhile.

The Forceful Personality Mate

In my work with clients, I have heard many married women say time and time again that they didn't know exactly what it was that made them fall in love with their partner. It was something intangible, indescribable. That he just "swept her off her feet." What I would venture to say is that her partner is a powerful person with a forceful personality. Each of us with more than a handful of women friends, relatives, or acquaintances can think of someone in a relationship with such a man. He's the one who may not physically be *GQ* material, but is usually surrounded by people who hang on his every word. People just gravitate to him. You know the type—the pied piper, the life of the party. He's the storyteller who can paint vivid pictures with his words, or the deep, philosophical one who can send your thoughts into recesses of your mind that you never knew existed. One client described being in her partner's presence as being "as close to a state of awakened hypnosis" as she could imagine. Her sentiments echoed those of Jackie, another smart, motivated woman who had a mate with a forceful personality.

Jackie grew up in a rundown inner-city neighborhood, the third daughter of immigrant parents. They instilled in her the necessity of being able to support herself and the belief that she would have to work for everything she got in life. They did not have the money to send her to college, so she worked at the Department of Water and Power during the day in order to put herself through paralegal school at night. Soon after completing her studies, she was hired to work in the office of the city's district attorney. She was on the way to creating the life she wanted for herself. She thought that perhaps she would meet a nice lawyer in the D.A.'s office and have the fairy-tale life that had eluded her parents.

A man came along, but he wasn't a lawyer in the D.A.'s office. In fact, she met him closer to her parent's home than to her job. His name was Carl.

Ironically, it was a long-standing tradition in Jackie's family that brought Jackie and Carl together for the first time. On the first Saturday of every month, Jackie's family gathered together for food and fellowship, the location rotating from one family member's home to another's. This particular month it was Jackie's parent's turn to host, and at the last minute Jackie's mother needed some things from the store. She asked Jackie to go to the neighborhood market and purchase them: Carl's market.

Carl was a suave, charismatic man who had opened a corner grocery store, a coin laundry, and a video rental store in Jackie's parents' neighborhood. He instantly became a respected figure in the community because he ran his businesses efficiently and he provided some much-needed services. Carl hired residents of the community to work in the new businesses, thus giving them a feeling that they had a personal stake in their success. This also served to keep them off the streets and out of trouble. His presence was a positive influence for the neighborhood.

Carl was working in the back office when he noticed Jackie enter the store on the closed-circuit security monitor. He was instantly struck by her beauty. Generally he did not work at the cash register, but this time he came out of the office and sent the cashier on duty on her break. As Jackie approached the register, he flashed a broad, warm smile.

"New to the neighborhood?" he inquired.

"No, I grew up here," she replied. "It's just that I'm always working and I usually do my shopping near my job."

"Sure would like to do something to change that. I'm Carl, the owner, and I haven't seen such a beautiful face since I started doing business here," he said.

Jackie felt flushed. "I just might have to consider making some changes in my shopping habits," she replied. She let out a hearty laugh and finished paying for her items. Carl walked her to the door and, in an attempt to score points, opened it for her. Jackie wasn't used to such chivalry, and it did make an impression on her. While it wasn't love at first sight, there was definitely something about Carl that Jackie found intriguing.

Jackie did change her shopping habits and frequented Carl's market more often. They became friends, and soon they were talking on the telephone fairly regularly. One day when she was in the market he finally said to her, "Since you won't ask me out, I've decided to ask you. What are you doing this Saturday night?"

"Oh, lots of exciting things like polishing my nails and watching TV," she responded sarcastically.

"Have you ever tried salsa dancing?" Carl asked.

"Yeah, I love it."

"Then what do you say about the two of us going dancing Saturday night?"

Jackie could hardly contain her excitement, but she managed to keep her wits about her and calmly replied, "That sounds like a date to me. What time shall I expect you?"

"Seven-thirty, and not a minute later. Oh—and don't forget to give me your address." Thus began the courtship of Jackie and Carl.

As their relationship evolved, Jackie not only fell in love with Carl, she also began to see him as the residents of the community did, as a kind of "godfather" type, a "prince" who came to make life better in the neighborhood and for her. She felt that Carl completed her. They eventually married and moved into their own home in the suburbs. Carl continued to run his market and other businesses in the inner-city neighborhood where Jackie grew up.

What Jackie never discovered until after she was married to Carl was that although the coin laundry and video store were legitimate businesses, he was selling more than groceries in the food market. The market was simply a front for his major source of income: peddling illegal government documents. Affluent college students came there to purchase fake identification cards. Anyone who needed a social security card, a passport, or birth certificate could obtain it from Carl. It was a very lucrative business.

When Jackie became suspicious and confronted him about it, he denied that he was doing anything illegal. He stated that he was simply providing assistance to people in need. Her intuition told her that wasn't the whole truth, but she ignored the voice inside of her. If it was true, she knew that her fairy-tale lifestyle, to which she had become so accustomed, would be threatened. That meant more to her than confronting Carl and risking the loss of it all. She did love him after all, and he was a very important member of her old community.

Even though she constantly felt uneasy about the things she suspected Carl was doing, he continually reassured her with his irresistible powers of persuasion that everything was kosher. She decided that she could learn to live with it as long as he was careful. A token of his appreciation every now and then such as a pair of flawless diamond stud earrings didn't hurt either. Besides, she had quit her job and become one of the "ladies who lunch," when the "grocery market" had begun to produce more money in one year than she made in three years working as a paralegal. She toyed with the idea of going to law school a few times, but

Carl hinted that doing so might take her away from him too often. She acquiesced.

Ironically, living a life of leisure began to take a toll on Jackie. In many ways she and Carl had achieved the American Dream. In contrast to the cramped duplex that her parents lived in, they had purchased a beautiful estate home that required hired help to keep it clean and maintained. She had more free time than she knew what to do with, so she simply began sleeping later every day. Some days she didn't bother to get out of bed at all. On those days, however, she would manage to get showered and dressed right before Carl got home from work. She hid her discontent well. She had everything that money could buy and a husband who loved and adored her. The only thing he asked of her was that she keep her nose out of his business dealings. What started out as mild blues escalated to a mild but unshakeable depression. Before long, she turned to the Internet as a source of relief. There she found solace in two things: online shopping and antidepressants, which were as easy to order as a new pair of shoes. She withdrew more and more, until the point that she simply felt numb.

Jackie communicated less and less with her parents and her old friends from the days when she worked as a paralegal. She quickly changed the subject when people made remarks about how lavishly she and Carl lived. The stress of keeping up the façade wore heavily on her. Shopping, once a pleasant escape, lost its ameliorative effect. Jackie was unaware that she, like so many other women in similar situations, was suffering from Powerful Mate Syndrome. All she knew was that she had gotten everything she had ever wanted—a faithful husband who was a good provider, a wonderful home, a great deal of disposable income, and the freedom to do whatever she pleased—and she was utterly miserable.

The powerful mate with a forceful personality doesn't have to be a loud, brash character who walks around wielding a baseball bat. In fact, he doesn't need weapons and he doesn't need ostentatious displays to declare his strength. He doesn't have be seven feet tall and weigh three hundred pounds to get the attention and respect of those around them. His strength lies in the force of his personality. He may not drive the most expensive car or wear a diamond-encrusted platinum watch or the latest designer clothing, but he is undeniably an alpha male. Such men, with all their natural charisma, are particularly difficult for PMS-prone women to resist.

The Sexy Mate

Using their sex appeal to gain advantage used to be a tactic utilized primarily by women. In fact, it was often the only real power some women had. But more and more, men are becoming aware of their ability to cash in on being sexy, too. Note the rise of the term *metrosexual*. Men are discovering that many of the things that women have been doing for ages to make themselves attractive will work for them, too. Facials, manicures, pedicures, body waxing, and a host of other services are now being added to men's "to do" lists. And while I think most women applaud the heightened level of attention that men are paying to themselves, what makes a man sexy to a woman will always be a highly subjective mix of characteristics.

Sexiness is not limited to what the eye can see, nor is there one standard by which all men are judged. For some women, sexiness is purely physical. For others, it entails something psychological or emotional. But for most of us it is a combination of both, and as we evolve, so too does our idea of what is sexy.

Even so, there is always that one man that women will generally agree is sexy. I don't mean the guy on the cover of *People* magazine's annual "Sexiest Man Alive" issue. That's reserved for people in show business. No, I'm talking about the man who does meaningful work that will improve life on the planet, goes bike riding a couple of times a week, and likes chocolate chip cookies with milk for breakfast every now and then—the average "Joe" you see every now and then in your day-to-day life who has something about him that fits not only your idea of sexy but a lot of other women's, too. It might be quirky or it might be common. Perhaps it's that guy with the dimples you see at the dog park with his three-legged dog. It may be the UPS man with the body of Adonis and the teeth that look like he just jumped out of a toothpaste commercial. Maybe it's the dad who teaches school all week and still makes time to referee his daughter's soccer games every weekend. Or perhaps it is your brother-in-law who makes his living as a carpenter but takes cooking lessons on the weekends so that he can learn to prepare gourmet meals for your sister. And let's not forget the guy who would rather spend a couple of hours on Saturday browsing through a bookstore than watching the latest "blow 'em up, shoot 'em up" flick in the movie theater.

The sexy mate, just like all the others, has a form of power. There is something about having a sexy mate, the one whom everyone else is looking at or trying to get the attention of, that can make his partner feel either validated (that she is the one with whom he has chosen to be) or insecure (that other women will attempt to "take him away" from her). This is particularly true if the man is generally deemed to be the sexier of the two. Having a sexy mate sometimes leads women to doubt their own sexiness. There again is the concept of measuring oneself by someone else's yardstick. Doubts and insecurities can begin to creep into the psyche of the partner of a sexy mate, and what once attracted a woman to her partner may begin to appear as a negative in her eyes. If he gets more attention than she does, she may either try to compete with his sexy image or, on the contrary, decide to keep as low a profile as possible. Neither reaction is a healthy one.

The point is, any one of us who has dated or been in a relationship with a sexy man knows the power of sexiness. Other women are attracted to it and other men are envious of it, and it would be naive to deny the power of a sexy mate. Barry is what I would consider to be a sexy mate. He graduated Phi Beta Kappa with a B.S. in environmental science. He was active in campus politics as the student body president and his extracurricular activities included singing in an a cappella group and teaching yoga part-time on campus. When Barry graduated from college he was inundated with job offers but he chose to strike out on his own and follow his heart.

That path led him to creating a wildlife refuge for animals and a school where children could learn how to explore the great outdoors safely. The refuge and the school were a tremendous success. Mothers with their young children, school groups, and even college students came to visit. Local television stations came to film stories about it. As impressive as the facility was, people were always most riveted by Barry's enthusiasm and knowledge.

Women in particular marveled at his patience with young children, and soon everyone was describing him as "sexy." It isn't that Barry is sexy by Hollywood standards. He's not. What makes him sexy are his confidence, his passion, and his kindness. Those are attributes that, in my opinion, are always sexy. And they can't be altered by what he is wearing, driving, or the number of credit cards in his wallet. Barry is constantly hit on by women who would like to have him as their mate. So far, he's been too busy saving animals and teaching children to fit an exclusive relationship into his life.

The bottom line is, there are many different types of powerful mates, and consequently many potential candidates for Powerful Mate Syndrome. Don't think that because your mate is not famous or filthy rich that you are not susceptible to PMS. Perhaps your mate is prominent in your community or a high achiever professionally. He may be one of the forceful personality types or a sexy mate. No matter which of the categories he fits into, or whether he fits into any of them, if you have a mate who you believe is powerful, you are vulnerable to PMS.

In the next chapter we will explore one of the major components of PMS—loss. It may be a difficult chapter for some of you to digest because it will force you to acknowledge all that you have lost in the process of attempting to attain the fairy tale. Take it in small bites. You do not need to consume it all in one sitting. The magnitude of it can be overwhelming and devastating. But you didn't come under the influence of the "Powerful Prince" messages all at once and neither will you be able to rid yourself of them in one fell swoop. Remember: You are not alone. I have gone through this process and I can assure you that you will emerge from it freed from the fantasy and empowered to create your own reality tale. Proceed and Prevail!

3

A HIGH PRICE TO PAY,
WITH HIDDEN COSTS

"Wherever I am, I am what is missing."
—MARK STRAND, *Keeping Things Whole*

LOSS IS AN issue central to Powerful Mate Syndrome. Not only does a woman with PMS feel as though her strength and purpose is lost, the feeling of being lost can extend into other areas of her life, such as her ability to exercise control over her financial situation. She may feel that she has no identity separate and apart from her mate. Her ability to connect authentically with her mate may become strained. The experience of these compound losses can be discombobulating for the woman affected and devastating to her mate and their relationship. In this chapter we'll be focusing on these six connected losses: of identity, self-worth, dreams and goals, financial power, authentic connection to one's mate, and of a sense of true feelings and purpose.

Loss of Identity

Generally when we talk about someone suffering from a loss of identity in a relationship we are referring to one partner in a relationship being overshadowed by some quality of the other, whether it is some level of fame or notoriety, the person's wealth, some extraordinary accomplishment, or, in this culture where we are so consumed with people's physical appearance, their beauty. But what about the woman whose entire sense of self comes from being someone's wife or girlfriend, rather than from anything they bring to the table? This even happens to a lot of women who are themselves talented and worthy of acknowledgment, especially if they happen to be in a social circle that has no appreciation for what they do and who they are as individuals. It is a situation that many women who are in relationships with powerful mates experience. And it is precisely this experience where the pull toward seeing one's mate as *all-powerful* creeps into the psyche.

Our first detour to the land of PMS comes when we begin looking for a mate to complete us rather than to complement us. I won't be the first person you will hear say that all of us are born whole, complete, and in the image of a perfect being. That doesn't mean we are perfect, but it does mean that it's time for us to stop entering into relationships as if we are defective. When we function from this kind of deficit thinking, we set ourselves up to believe that we need another person to make us whole, rather than to add to what already exists about us that is good, wholesome, capable, and complete.

Becoming Stand-Alone Women

I recently had dinner with two of my closest friends. Halfway through our meal I looked around the table and thought about what it was that we all have in common. The first thing was that each of us is a mother. One friend has four children. The other has two children, and I have my two girls. A great deal of our pride and identity comes from being parents. But the second and most poignant thing that we have in common is that each of us at one time was married to a powerful man who was the star of the relationship. Our relationships each ended under different circumstances, but I have dubbed us "the survivors of the three Ds": death, desertion, and divorce. We are all college-educated, middle-class women who took different paths but ended up at the same destination. Each of us counted on our mates to give us our identity, and when they were no longer there, neither were we—at least not psychologically. Frankly, I remember feeling as though I weren't there physically either. Each of us had to launch our own individual salvage operation or else go quietly into the night. When you have children, though, there is no such thing as going quietly into the night. Even if you feel like lying down and dying, you have to go on, no matter how daunting the task seems. I think my friends would agree when I say that none of us is used to doing anything quietly, the one exception being in our relationships with our now-departed mates. It's incredible how Powerful Mate Syndrome can make a mouse out of the most opinionated, action-oriented woman, so entrenched are those "Powerful Prince" impulses. In our relationships, the three of us left it up to our princes to define our identity and, lo and behold, we all ended up with serious cases of PMS. When our mates died, divorced, and deserted us, we were left wondering who we were. We were forced to become what we should have been all along: "stand-alone" women.

I'm not suggesting that women should not be involved in relationships. Not at all. Just that becoming "stand-alone" women capable of living our lives and defining our identities separate from a significant other person, knowing who we are, *whether or not we are in a relationship,* is the ideal. In short, a "stand-alone" woman doesn't feel that she should become insignificant because she has a significant other. Her identity is derived from within. It is built on her values and her interests, and it is solid. It remains largely unaffected by the presence or absence of a mate.

Even if neither your marriage nor your mate shows signs of ill health, you can't know what each day will bring. It might be an ordinary day, filled with the usual activities and routines or it could turn out to be a day that alters your life forever.

My dinner companion Dana became a widow suddenly when her husband was shot during a bank robbery. That day started out the same as any other, with Matt having breakfast and saying good-bye to her and their son and daughter. He called Dana at 10:45 that morning, as he always did, just before he left to do some banking. She did not realize that it would be the last time they would ever speak. Had Matt gone to the bank on the day before or a few hours later, he might still be alive today. We'll never know. What we do know for sure is that when Dana buried Matt, she also buried the source of her identity. She was faced not only with her very real grief for her husband, but with the need to begin constructing a whole new life based on who she was and who she was going to be in the world, rather than based on being Matt's wife and her children's mom. It wasn't until Matt was cremated that she realized how much she had erased herself from their story.

Fortunately for my friend Dana, she was able to construct a new identity for herself remarkably quickly. The very first thing she did was to get herself and her children into therapy. She wrote a business plan to take her cute but fledgling yoga studio to new heights. Then she found a fitness boot camp and started attending it three times a week. And she reaffirmed her commitment to her spiritual growth.

Out of her great and tragic loss, Dana forged a powerful "stand-alone" identity. She found love again with a powerful man who also has a "stand-alone" identity. Together they are an awesome duo. They are the epitome of what is possible when a powerful "stand-alone" woman connects with a powerful "stand-alone" partner. I am willing to bet that no matter what happens to or with Dana's mate, she won't suffer from Powerful Mate Syndrome again.

My other friend, Natalie, along with her four children, was deserted by her husband, Oliver. One Fourth of July he got in his brand new Escalade, telling her he was going to the gas station to fill the propane tank for the barbeque grill, and never returned. Several weeks later, after an exhaustive search by the police, Natalie learned that he simply had decided to move across town to live with a woman with whom he had been committing adultery and had sired another child. He has seen his and Natalie's children one time in the past five years.

Natalie is one of those women who is so beautiful it leaves

you speechless. She has that effect on men and women alike. She is five-foot-four and has a figure that rivals any supermodel you can think of. And here's one more reason to envy her: She is also a member of MENSA. So how does a woman with seemingly so much going for her end up with a loser like Oliver? Because an intelligent, beautiful, and motivated woman like Natalie grows up being bombarded with the "Powerful Prince" message, and someone like Oliver, charismatic and cunning, successful in his career but lacking in character, and a master of deception comes along and triggers that embedded desire to be someone's princess. In short, Natalie, like me, became afflicted with Powerful Mate Syndrome and she, also like me, took the super-deluxe journey through the land of PMS. We each lost our identities in that of the person to whom we were married.

When her husband walked out the door, that propane tank that he took with him might as well have been Natalie's identity. She had spent most of her adult life being a spokesperson for his line of health and nutritional products. Although her own accomplishments and interests had been numerous before she became his princess, everyone knew her as "Oliver's wife." She had lost her separate self. Now that the Prince had revealed himself as a toad, what was she to do?

I'll tell you what she did. She felt down and depressed for a little while. She even ate a few too many cookies while she was having her pity party. (It's okay to have a few cookies, though my personal recommendation is chocolate!) When she got done with the cookies, she got angry. Anger can be a useful emotion if it spurs us to do the things we need to do for ourselves. Next, she hired a great divorce attorney (yes, there are a few of them out there). Because Natalie has a strong attachment to her church, she and her children became active members of a church support group for families experiencing separation and divorce. While the support group did not have the strict confidentiality rules that would have been in place had she gone to a therapist, she felt safe and cared for there. Everyone in the church knew about the situation anyway, and she certainly hadn't done anything to be ashamed of.

Natalie had a gargantuan task in front of her. She actually had five new identities to help rebuild. Not only was her own identity decimated, but her four children's self-worth was greatly affected by Oliver's abandonment as well. Last, but certainly not least, Natalie had to rebuild a work identity. She proved again how smart she really was by going back to school at night to study chemistry. She took what she learned in those classes and her interest in women's beauty products and created a line of skin-care products. Next, she found a venture capitalist who believed in her products and put up the capital to launch her line. She now has thirteen products available. They have been tremendously successful, and she plans to introduce more products to the line in the near future. The business generates enough income to employ six full-time employees, as well as to comfortably support her lifestyle, send all of her children to top-notch private schools, and, most important, to sleep at night knowing that if Oliver never sends another child-support check, she and her children will be perfectly fine. It took Natalie nearly three years to create her new life as single mother, chemist, entrepreneur, and a "stand-alone" woman. She juggled the schedules of her four children, which often were all different, classes at night, which meant that she had to depend on church members to baby-sit at times, homework—both hers and the kids'—and the trials and tribulations of starting a new business. Fortunately, there was the Small Business Administration, which provided mentoring and support for her during the start-up phase of the business. She also found a staunch supporter in her venture capitalist.

Still, there were days when she would ask the rhetorical question, like we all do at one time or another, "Why me?" Then she would tell herself that if Oliver hadn't walked out that day, she would still be in that façade of a marriage, she would still be just "Oliver's wife," her children would have had a toad instead of a man as their role model for what a father is, and she would not have the fulfilling work and lucrative source of income that she had created for herself. Laying claim to her life, her identity, and her happiness was worth the three years it took to accomplish.

Natalie took what appeared to be Nothing and turned it into Something. But I find it regrettable that it often takes a devastating event to spur women like myself and my friends Dana and Natalie into action. If we had come to our relationships with an awareness that our deep-seated desires to be "the princess" are fantasies, coupled with the knowledge that we do not have to lose ourselves to find someone who will love us, there would be many fewer cases of Powerful Mate Syndrome wreaking havoc in the lives of women and their partners.

Loss of Self-Worth

Very much connected to a loss of identity is a loss of self-worth. When I was growing up I dealt with many of the same self-esteem and self-worth issues as most other women. I thought that I was too skinny and longed to have a bigger, fuller derriere like the girl Tonya who lived down the street from me. She was the quintessence of beauty in my neighborhood and the object of all the boys' attention. There was a gap between my front teeth that a train could have passed through. Then, at the age of nine, I was jumping on my bed, fell off of it, and chipped one of my front teeth on the side rail. That didn't do anything to enhance my looks. My childhood was filled with insecurities and things I wanted to change about myself, but even with all that, I still believed that I was valued by my family and friends. I felt good about myself. I was an achiever throughout high school and was headed for college so that I could go on to achieve my goals.

So where did the loss of self-worth begin? How is it that I am entering the second half of my life not having accomplished half of the things I knew, before I was the age of sixteen, that I was destined to do? What happened in the two decades between then and now?

I'll tell you what happened. I met and fell in love with someone who tapped into my dormant desire to be rescued and made to feel like a princess. I thought that I had found the embodiment of my fantasy prince. And he was, according to the world's standards, worth more than I was: He had found a means of self-expression that the world valued and rewarded with great adulation and large sums of money. As I compared what the world said about him to what I had accomplished, I arrived at the conclusion that he was somebody and I was nobody. Sadly, at the age of twenty-two, I had not learned what I have now come to know so well: You cannot measure your life by anyone else's yardstick.

There are many things in life that we can survive and even thrive without having, but self-worth is not one of them. Without it, there is not much left to lose. Sure, many of us are good at faking it. For years I managed to keep up the façade of the happy, fulfilled wife of a successful professional athlete. However, when we give all our energy to putting on a show for others rather than being authentic about our feelings, we siphon off our essence, the very life force of who we are. That's certainly what happened to me. I doubt that many people knew how poorly I felt about myself, because I never complained and I never neglected my outer appearance. Still, I was utterly miserable, because all that window dressing was hanging on the human mannequin I had become. I shudder to think how many women with powerful partners are waging that same battle to keep up the façade that their self-worth is happily intact. Isn't it ironic that James's last name is Worthy? Let me tell you, when I married him I might have attached the name Worthy to mine, but the last thing I felt was *worthy*. Looking back from the vista that hindsight provides, I can trace the beginnings of my loss of self-worth to the beginning of my marriage.

Even though Los Angeles is a huge city, it is in a lot of ways a very small town. Lakers fans love their team and they want to know everything they can learn about them. If you can believe it, early in my marriage I drove around with a license plate frame that read, "I am Worthy of James." That's how proud I was of being his wife. People would often ride up next to me and wave or honk the horn. Of course now I can see that it just illustrates how misdirected my attention was. Nothing says better than that frame how much

I used James as the barometer of my self-worth. The misperception that James was more powerful than I was, that my self-worth was dependent on him, and that I had to be less than he was had taken complete hold of my psyche. Had I had a strong sense of my own self-worth, that license plate frame might have read, "Is James Worthy of Me?" That may sound arrogant, but imagine what a statement it would have made.

A brilliant psychologist named Dr. Judith Bin-Nun once said to me, "Be who you are." Those four little words that hit me with such impact are the first step in safeguarding your self-worth. *Be who you are and let your mate be who he is.* Never mind what the world, your mother-in-law, or your neighbors think about how wonderful, incredible, or irresistible he is. They don't get a vote about your life.

Every day I became a little less than what I should be, less than what I knew I could be, and it was the most frustrating and inexplicable thing. I could not figure out how to turn around the feeling that I was trapped on a sinking ship.

Are you convinced that you are nobody without your mate? Are you wondering what happened to the person you were before you became involved in your relationship? Did you think that your perception of him as a prince who chose *you* to be his princess would result in you feeling more powerful? Did the opposite happen? Are you feeling like less than a whole person? These are all feelings common to women whose self-worth has been eroded by Powerful Mate Syndrome. I have seen it in my clients, my friends, and I have had strangers tell me their experiences with similar feelings.

This is not a fairy tale so I cannot wave a magic wand and instantly restore your self-worth, but then remember you didn't lose it in one brief moment either. The good news is that not only can self-worth be restored, you can use this opportunity to take it to a higher level where it will be able to withstand all future assaults on it. We will cross that bridge in Part Three—The Reclamation.

For now, simply take heart: What has been lost can be restored.

Loss of Dreams and Goals

"There are many ways of breaking a heart. Stories are full of hearts broken by love, but what really breaks a heart is taking away its dream—whatever that dream might be."

—PEARL S. BUCK

Another loss that tends to intertwine with the loss of self-worth is the loss of one's own dreams and goals. I can't tell you how many women married to powerful mates simply give up their own dreams as they lose themselves to their powerful princes.

Amy's story provides a good example. Amy had a lot of dreams when she married her college sweetheart, Jay. They met in college at an audition for an all-campus variety show. He was doing stand-up comedy and she was performing with a band she had formed with three other students. Both acts were accepted for the show and were big hits with the crowd. After that night, Amy and Jay became inseparable, even though their schedules often had them going in entirely different directions. Jay began to make a name for himself in some of the local comedy clubs and occasionally traveled to nearby cities for appearances. Amy's band was also on the rise. It developed a small but loyal following and even cut its first CD in her senior year. It seemed as though they both had bright futures ahead of them in the entertainment business.

After graduation, Amy and Jay moved to Seattle. It was a large enough city to provide work opportunities for both of them, yet not so large that they would not be able to get a foot in the door, as might be the case in Los Angeles or New York. The members of Amy's band were also willing to make the move to Seattle, which meant that they could carry on without missing a beat. Life was good for both Amy and Jay. He worked regularly and was starting to create a reputation for himself. He had a feeling that it was only a matter of time until some manager from a big city would come calling.

Amy's band took off like wildfire in Seattle and the surrounding areas. She and her band mates were fast-rising stars. All her life she had dreamed of having a career performing in front of people, and now it seemed as if it were finally coming within her reach. She traveled with the band several weeks out of the month, but since she and Jay had no children, not even pets, she didn't see any problem with it. As often as her schedule permitted, she would go to Jay's performances to show her support for his career. No matter how busy her career kept her, she was still madly in love with Jay.

On the Seattle scene, they were becoming a celebrity couple, and they began to experience the lack of privacy that comes with success in the entertainment business. Interestingly it was Jay, Mr. Stand-up Comedy himself, who liked the attention the least. Amy loved it and figured that it could only help increase her band's exposure. Either way, they were happily married and they both derived great satisfaction from their careers.

Then came the event that changed everything. Amy and her band were the cover story for a national rock music publication. It was their first national exposure. The cover photograph was of the entire band, but Amy was featured prominently in front, as was to be expected. It was an awesome photo and the copies of the magazine practically flew off the newsstands. Amy bought seventy-five copies to send to her friends and family members around the country. The magazine even sent her a framed copy to hang in her home. Amy was walking on air. Her dreams were coming true and now she had proof that she could hold in her hands.

Amy thought it was curious that Jay's enthusiasm over her great fortune seemed watered down at best. After all, hadn't they spent many nights telling each other their dreams and vowing to support the other through thick and thin? Everything was perfect but moving so quickly. Amy dismissed his nonchalance as simply fatigue from his own schedule, which was gathering momentum as well.

One night both Amy and Jay had gigs. Jay finished up before Amy and went over to the nightclub to catch her last set. The club was filled to capacity. The fans were rabid. The excitement was palpable. He was actually taken aback by the intensity. Amy and 333 Possibilities put on an incredible show. They were so good that the fans demanded two encores. By the time Amy and Jay got home it was nearly four o'clock in the morning. Jay mixed gin and tonic cocktails while Amy headed straight for the shower. When she returned, he handed her a cocktail and she sidled up next to him on the buttery leather couch.

Then he announced, without any emotion in his voice or change in his demeanor, that he had been doing some thinking and had come to the conclusion that he could not have a wife in show business. Amy felt as though she was Wile E. Coyote in a Looney Tunes cartoon just after he's been hit by a train. But, unlike Wile E. who gets up immediately, dusts himself off, and is back to his old tricks in the next minute, Amy felt as though she had shattered into a million pieces. She wondered who was going to come along and sweep her up.

Amy was blindsided; she couldn't begin to figure out where this pronouncement had come from. How could he fix his mouth to say such a thing, and what motivated it, she wondered? Wasn't this the same person who had shared her dreams of making it? Wasn't this the same person who had seen her perform in front of thousands of people each week and who knew, more than anyone, the exhilaration that performing brought her? Was this what she got in return for her support of his career, both emotionally and with her presence, through the highs and lows, in good times and in bad? What about the two months that she didn't perform at all in order to nurse him back to health after he fell off their roof and broke both of his legs? Why didn't she deserve the same right as Jay to make her dreams come true?

But she didn't say a word. It was like an out-of-body experience for Amy. An instantaneous blanket of shock and depression enveloped her. There she was, with the man who she thought was her prince denying her his blessing to pursue the thing that she had wanted long before she'd ever met him: her music career. They attempted to engage in a conversation about what was essentially an ultimatum. He confessed that he felt uncomfortable about all the men who came to her shows leering at her. He said he was "afraid of what could happen" between her "and an admiring fan."

What made no sense to Amy was that she had demonstrated her complete faith in his fidelity while he traveled and worked all over the country, in and out of hotels, but he couldn't bring himself to trust her while she did her job. Amy felt as though her commitment to Jay, their marriage, and, most of all, her integrity was being questioned. The gin and tonic was beginning to make her sluggish, and Amy felt as though she had heard all that she could tolerate in one sitting, so she ended the conversation abruptly by agreeing not to pursue her career any further. But she was lying to herself and Jay. And though Amy was not aware of it then, that night the seeds of deception and deep resentment were sown. In the following days, Amy tried to convince herself that she meant it. Deep down, though, she was livid. How dare he demand that she give up her music aspirations? Hell, he traveled more than she did! Didn't comedians have groupies just like musicians?

About a week after Jay's big pronouncement, he went on the road for a two-week tour and Amy began to live what was basically a double life. She told Jay that she was no longer performing but it was not true. Luckily for her, Jay was traveling all the time now. She would simply wait for him to leave town or lie to him about what she was doing and continue to play her gigs. Because there was no consistency in his schedule, sometimes she would miss practices, and occasionally she was a no-show. This created some anger among her band members, but no one could do what Amy did nearly as well, so they hung in there with her. Amy hated what she was doing but she felt as though it was the lesser of two evils. The greater one would have been to give up her career altogether. She could not believe the extremes she had to go through to pursue a perfectly legitimate dream. It would have been understandable if she had been pursuing a career as an adult film star, but this just didn't make sense.

Other than her band members, Amy didn't have a support system in place in Seattle. She began to internalize the feelings of anger, betrayal, and overwhelming loss that constantly flooded her mind. She didn't feel as though she could talk to Jay about her feelings, and their communication, as well as other aspects of their relationship, suffered. Amy withdrew more and more from Jay, who she now saw as her oppressor. A chill fell over their relationship and their household. Eventually, Amy gave up the band altogether because she felt that she was betraying both Jay and their relationship. The double life she was leading left her tired and feeling like she was always on the edge. But quitting sent her *over* the edge. Now her conversations with Jay were limited to passing exchanges and unimportant daily details. Jay worked as much as possible, but Amy did not attend his shows. She spent her days watching MTV and VH1. Then she decided to start bringing home animals that she would find either roaming the streets of Seattle or from the animal shelter. She stopped when the tally stood at thirteen cats, three mixed-breed dogs, a bird, an iguana, and a couple of blind, geriatric guinea pigs. Amy was slipping further into her depression, which was not helped by the fact that every night she would attempt to soothe herself by taking a few shots of gin from a bottle that she kept hidden in her medicine cabinet. Just making it from one day to the next soon became her biggest goal in life. One day she was channel surfing and she saw her old band's first music video on MTV. This sent her into a deep funk. Jay, having become weary of living with the fallout of his ultimatum, finally suggested that Amy see a medical doctor about her depression and that perhaps they should find a family therapist to help them salvage their marriage. She did go to her physician who immediately prescribed an antidepressant for her. He was also able to recommend an experienced family therapist.

You can see that Amy had more than just PMS to contend with. Not only was she plagued by the loss of her dreams and goals, she also had to deal with her "Powerful Prince," who felt threatened by her power and talents. There are so many women like Amy who stop short of their dreams and goals because they don't feel as though they have the power to persevere. Amy questioned (in her own mind) why she didn't have the right to pursue her career, but she did not bring her questions up in discussions with Jay, which is where they belonged.

As mean and selfish as Jay's ultimatum was, Jay was actually not the problem. Why? For two reasons. First, Jay simply made a statement. Yes, inherent in the statement was the demand that Amy abandon her dream, but did he say, "Quit or I will kill you"? No. Amy might have *thought* not complying would (figuratively, at least) kill Jay, or she might have felt that her own anguish about going against his wishes would kill her. But all of that is fear and fantasy. There wasn't some big bad ogre who would destroy their marriage had she chosen to challenge Jay rather than be the obedient princess who follows orders. The worst thing that might have happened eventually was that she might have lost Jay. But considering how the loss of her dream essentially cost her her health, I'm not sure that losing Jay would have been a worse choice.

Yes, Jay was selfish and narrow-minded, and he did betray her in a way, but ultimately the problem lay in the way that Amy chose to respond. When it comes right down to it, our responses are the only thing that we have real power over. In fact, Amy did not have to acquiesce, lie, or go through the machinations necessary to carry on a double life. She had a choice.

To stand up for yourself is not an easy thing to do when you have been conditioned to be a princess. On the contrary, you believe that the prince is dominant and his desires are the ones that matter most. But you cannot give up your dreams and goals because your mate has an issue with his own self-worth and doesn't understand what it is that you need to make your life its optimum. In *A Return to Love,* Marianne Williamson expressed this most eloquently:

Our deepest fear is not that we are inadequate. Our deepest fear is that we are powerful beyond measure. It is our light, not our darkness, that frightens us. We ask ourselves, who am I to be brilliant, gorgeous, talented and fabulous? Actually, who are you not to be? You are a child of God. Your playing small doesn't serve the world. There is nothing enlightened about shrinking so that other people won't feel insecure around you. . . . As we let our light shine, we unconsciously give other people permission to do the same.

As we are liberated from our own fears, our presence automatically liberates others.

Amy did not need to snuff out her light. In fact, doing so did not empower her, Jay, or their marriage. Yes, they had issues that they needed help dealing with, but those were not going to go away simply because Amy quit making music. After all, the music was never the problem. If it had been, then it would have come up during their college years together. The only thing that changed was Amy's level of success. In Amy and Jay's case, I would actually say they *both* suffered from Powerful Mate Syndrome. And that, as they say, is a "double whammy." No matter how much trouble Jay had with Amy's success, the answer did not lie in giving up her dreams. It never does.

Loss of Financial Power

Powerful Mate Syndrome enables women to hang onto the belief that if they are nice, beautiful, and compliant—all the things a princess is—then they will attract the prince who can make their world not only go round, but up and down, sideways, and diagonally. It does not say anything about money. You are simply fooling yourself if you don't believe that money and financial power make the world go round. Cinderella never had to worry about paying a mortgage; she lived in the prince's castle, which, incidentally, was paid for by the prince's subjects! No, "Cindy" never had to worry about buying a car; she had the royal carriage. And if by chance something happened to it she could simply summon her fairy godmother who would magically appear and, with the use of her magic wand, turn a pumpkin into a carriage and take a couple of old rats and change them into horses! That's Cinderella's life, honey, not yours. Take it from Bella, a young woman who married her prince and assumed that she did not have to worry about the money because her prince had it all under control.

Bella and Trey were what a lot of people might consider a modern fairy-tale couple, except that Bella had a thriving career of her own. She did not expect that her husband, Trey, would create a life for her that would be perfect. But what she did buy into was the notion that he, being her idea of the modern-day prince—well-educated, motivated, handsome, employed—would and should have dominion over their family finances. It was an old belief that the women in her family had subscribed to for generations. The underlying belief was that to do otherwise—that is, for the woman to "meddle" in the financial affairs of the family—was emasculating for the man.

Both Bella and Troy were physicians. She was a pediatric oncologist and a published author. He was an ophthalmologist, specializing in laser surgery procedures. They both produced hefty incomes. They pooled all their financial resources and at first they kept most of their money in a simple interest-bearing account. Once they began to amass considerable amounts of cash, however, they decided to hire professional help. They interviewed four licensed financial planners and decided on Jack. Jack worked independently. He did not have ties to any large brokerage firms or banks and his overhead was low. He had a great track record in dealing with other people's money and came very highly recommended by his current clients, many of whom were billionaires. Even though their nest egg was smaller, they felt as though he would give them just as much time and consideration as he did his wealthier clients.

After Jack was retained by Bella and Trey, Bella bowed out of the financial picture, leaving things to Trey and Jack.

Jack managed their financial situation extremely well over the next four years. He set up a system to simplify payment of their monthly bills, but he did not have the authority to sign checks and never suggested it. In fact, he always insisted that Bella or Trey sign checks so that they would know exactly to whom and where their money was going. But signing checks was pretty much all they had to do.

As Trey and Bella became more financially secure, Trey began to pursue his golf hobby in his free time. He joined Coast Castle Country Club, which was known for having young movers and shakers as members rather than the old-money, stuffy types who frequently frown upon the nouveau riche. He and Bella were warmly welcomed by the membership. Bella, however, rarely frequented the club; but by reworking his schedule Trey found time to play golf three days a week.

It was on the links at Coast Castle that he met Glen, Steve, and Victor. They were all bachelors and always together at the club. Glen, Steve, and Victor were partners in a business that they called the GSV Consortium. As they became better acquainted with Trey, they shared more information about their operation, their clients, and their mission. They described themselves as one-third legal advisors, which was Victor's area of expertise; one-third public relations experts, which was Glen's area of expertise; and financial planning wizards, which was Steve's area of expertise. Their impassioned talks about their business convinced Trey that these guys were heavy-hitters.

The four of them spent many hours golfing and having drinks at the club, and they even began to see each other socially outside of Coast Castle. Soon Trey was talking to the guys about his practice, his family, and eventually his finances. He told them about his long history with Jack and complained that Jack was very conservative in his investment strategies and was not a particularly lively character, either. His friends were very sympathetic.

One day Trey informed Bella that he had terminated the relationship with Jack and now Glen, Steve, and Victor would be doing everything Jack had done plus more. Glen, the public relations guru, had some ideas about how to raise Trey's community profile and create more opportunities to advance his career. Steve would be handling everything in the realm of money and finances. Trey assured Bella that Steve had worked for some high-profile clients before, and that all she needed to do was sit back and relax. She needn't even worry about signing the monthly checks because Steve would now be authorized to sign on their account. Bella was somewhat skeptical about leaving Jack and replacing him with this trio of fast-talking operators. However, the belief she'd grown up with that the man is the lord of his castle and that the woman keeps her hands out of the money overrode the feeling in her gut that all wasn't on the up-and-up with this new situation.

One day about two years after the GSV Consortium had taken over their financial affairs, Bella was pulling into her garage when she noticed a tow truck parked a few doors down. She assumed that one of her neighbors was having car problems and just pulled in and went on about her business as usual. No more than three minutes later the doorbell rang. She looked through the security peephole but did not recognize the man standing there wearing some kind of official-looking jumpsuit. Nevertheless, she opened the door. "Ma'am, are you Bella Smith?"

"Yes," she replied cautiously. "What can I do for you?"

"I'm here to repossess that BMW that just pulled into your garage."

Bella thought that this had to be some kind of joke of Trey's. "You can't be serious," she replied.

The tow truck driver handed her some papers, which revealed that the car payments had not been made for the past three months. She attempted to reach someone in the office of the GSV Consortium, since this had been Steve's responsibility, but no one answered. Next she called Trey, who was just about to leave the office for the country club. She informed him that he had better come home because things much more urgent than golf needed his attention.

The repossession of the car was just the first in a long list of things that were mishandled by the partners of the GSV Consortium. Steve had also paid their house mortgage payments forty-five days late on six occasions the past year. He had also failed to mail their property taxes, which resulted in a lien being placed on their home. It turned out that the new H2 Hummers that each of the partners was driving were compliments of the checking account of Trey and Bella. It took Trey several months to uncover all the damage that had been done to their finances. Their cash reserves had been siphoned off for all kinds of miscellaneous, unaccounted-for expenses. Their accounts had been moved to a bank where the manager, Biff, was a close friend of Glen, Steve, and Victor's. Both Bella and Trey ended up with several negative items on their credit report.

And where was Bella in all this? Right where she had been the whole time—at home, in her place, keeping silent. It took some major financial and life overhauling to finally get themselves back on track financially. They had to give up their membership in the Coast Castle Country Club. They also considered pursuing criminal charges against Glen, Steve, and Victor, but after consulting with an attorney they came to the conclusion that doing so would be cost prohibitive. Plus, they didn't want a public airing of their naiveté and gullibility.

Through this experience, Bella learned that it was time to put an end to the old family tradition that had led her to turn a blind eye to her family's financial matters. She insisted that they eat their humble pie and go back to Jack to manage their financial matters. This time however, Bella and Trey met with him on the first Friday of every month to review everything about their financial situation. They had to close all kinds of accounts—checking, credit cards, and lines of credit that Steve had opened and that all of the members of the firm had used at one time or another. They ended up having to sell their beautiful Southwestern adobe home and downsize to a more modest and affordable place, but at least they still had their family intact. Bella had finally learned the high cost of being a princess. Her happy ending came about only as a result of her shedding the old ideas and putting into practice some new ones that truly fit her needs.

Bella is a prime example of someone with lots of money but no financial power. Of course women lose or give up their financial power in lots of ways, and we have to start turning that around. For starters, we women, especially those of us married to powerful mates, have to get over the idea that our princes can or should have exclusive domain over the money. If you can read, you can learn how to do the basics. If you can count, you're another step further down the road to handling the finances. And if you are really motivated to become what I call "the captain of your own financial ship," there are books, seminars, workshops, home-study courses, and computer programs—and, of course, there are always classes at your local community college or university. If a woman can go to the moon and back, be the managing editor of a large, prestigious newspaper, or be the national security advisor to the president of the United States, then surely the rest of us can learn how to keep up with our money! More important than keeping up with it is keeping it, period. We know that most women outlive their partners. Do you want to run the risk of having the only person who knows about your finances sitting in an urn on your fireplace mantle? Can you imagine having to have a séance to find out whether or not you have enough money to live on for the rest of your life? You simply can't afford to bury your head in the sand. The price may be way too high.

Loss of Authentic Connection to Your Mate

If you still think that having the fairy tale is the life for you, ask yourself just one question: "Do I want to be a princess or a real person?" The truth is, you cannot be both. A princess only gets to be compliant and look a certain way. She has to fit a mold; she doesn't get to break it or to create a new one. Think about it. What kind of connection did Cinderella have to her prince except that her foot fit into some shoe? Can't you just see the prince and princess appearing at a modern-day press conference to announce their engagement? Here's the reporter asking, "Your Highness, what was the thing that drew the two of you together?" To which the prince replies, "Her beauty and her foot." Does he say, "her compassion for people, her love of hunting, her great wisdom and intellectual prowess, the way she commands the respect of others" or anything of substance? No, he doesn't, because the princess image is based on what is on the surface, not on substance. Princess or person? You choose!

One of the most interesting phenomena that happens in relationships where PMS is at work is the loss of an authentic connection. It may be there at the start, but then it fades. Take Ellie and Harvey. They met at a Sierra Club outing for singles. They both love to travel and be outdoors. Harvey is a successful designer and manufacturer of skateboards and skateboarding apparel. Ellie has two jobs. She works as a cashier in a natural foods market and also works as a volunteer for a nonprofit animal rights organization. They hit it off famously on the outing and began dating each other exclusively very shortly thereafter. In the couple of years that passed, they both came to believe that they were meant to be life partners. They decided that they would get married in a simple ceremony on the beach with a few close friends and family members in attendance. Ellie and Harvey agreed that they should keep Harvey's house and live there since it was large and centrally located in the city.

For the first year or so, life was good for the newlyweds.

Harvey's business continued to grow and Ellie continued to work at the food store and as a volunteer. Harvey's work involved some travel to sports equipment trade shows and conventions across the country. He had even begun to do business in some Asian and European markets, which required international travel, and even though Harvey always stressed that these trips were not especially glamorous, Ellie found herself wanting to go anyway. "Surely things had to be more exciting on the road than in a food market," she surmised. What started out as an occasional trip with Harvey soon turned into a regular thing, with Ellie going on every trip. As the business grew and the trips became more frequent, Harvey and Ellie participated in fewer and fewer of the Sierra Club activities. Ellie was fired from her job at the food market because she spent more time away from the job than the management would tolerate. Now she was down to her one job as a volunteer for the nonprofit organization. She was very much committed to its mission, but her work with it mostly consisted of telephone solicitations for donations and stuffing envelopes for mailings. There was not a lot about it that was intellectually stimulating. Nevertheless, it did fit in with her life of travel with Harvey.

Ellie began to forge friendships with the wives of some of the other sporting goods dealers whom they would see at each of the different venues. The men would hawk their goods and the women would shop, dine, and visit the local day spa during the daylight hours. In the evenings, they would attend the large dinner that was normally a part of the convention or show. It all became quite routine. Ellie looked forward to seeing the girlfriends she had come to know and care about, but none of them seemed to have much going on in their lives except trotting around behind their husbands.

One day, while they were in Maui at a big sporting-goods show, Ellie and three of her "sporting-goods posse" friends decided they would spend the day luxuriating at the fabulous spa at the Grand Wailea Hotel. It was one of the most wonderful spas she had ever visited. However, in the middle of an exquisite body-wrap treatment, it suddenly occurred to her that the plastic wrap she was cocooned in felt a lot like her relationship with Harvey: It contained her and yet it cut her off from him.

She was flooded with thoughts about how she was with him virtually twenty-four hours a day, seven days a week. She hardly did anything apart from him or that didn't have some connection with his work. Their conversations always centered on the business or his business associates or the travel plans for the next venue. Lying there, she realized that she had a life of luxury, she was always with her beloved Harvey, and he adored her, but they had lost the authentic connection that they had shared when she was generating her own "scripts" for her life and sharing them with Harvey. Now they had one script: to promote and grow the business. Harvey made the money; Ellie enjoyed spending it. While there is nothing inherently wrong with spending money, it didn't provide Ellie with anything of substance in her life. How often had a conversation about the great swimsuit she purchased or the fantastic facial she had experienced help establish intimacy with Harvey? Never. All they had now was small talk. They didn't get out into nature and let go of concerns about the business anymore. They did not take time away from their business trips to vacation alone. Ellie had her fairy tale, but she had lost her authentic connection to Harvey. She had completely morphed into a princess. She had shed that person who had a life of her own, money of her own, and interests of her own. She had shed all the things that Harvey had initially found so attractive about her. Sure, she still had her wholesome face, but that was about all that remained of "the authentic Ellie." She had become a Cinderella clone.

Now there would have been nothing wrong with Ellie becoming a Cinderella clone, had it been a conscious decision and something that fit her vision of herself. But it didn't, and therein lay the problem. Ellie unknowingly became a PMS sufferer. She came to believe that being Harvey's princess was her calling in life. He could provide for her every need and she could simply ride his wave. As so often turns out to be the case, that one wave is not great enough to carry two people. While she lay there on the spa table, wrapped in warm seaweed mousse and plastic wrap, that wave crashed over Ellie. She realized that she had some work to do to get *herself* back. She didn't want to be Harvey's princess. She wanted to be his confidante, lover, friend, and partner. She wanted him to think she was interesting and challenging.

A princess, by definition, does not get to be her partner's confidante and partner. She is always subordinate, which bars having an authentic connection. Ellie decided that the cost of being a princess to herself and, more importantly, to her relationship with Harvey was one that she was not willing to pay. She loved the trips and travel. She also loved seeing all the friends that she had made through the years. But she loved Harvey more and cherished her relationship with him more than any of the perks of being a tagalong wife. She resolved that as soon as she was done with her seaweed body wrap she was going to make reservations for dinner for two that night and she would begin to share with Harvey the things that had been revealed to her about herself and their relationship that afternoon at the spa.

Ellie was taking the first steps on her journey to reestablishing her authentic connection to Harvey. She figured out that the bricks and mortar of her relationship to the partner she loved were in need of shoring up. She wanted the magic back in her relationship and realized that she didn't have to be a princess to have it. "Magic" can be created. It isn't just the stuff of fairy tales, but *you do have to create it.* You have to take responsibility for creating the magic in your relationship by being observant of what is actually occurring and being careful not to fall for mere illusions. Just being together doesn't mean that you and your partner are intimately connected. Watch carefully; don't be one of the women who find that her authentic connection to her mate has done a disappearing act.

Loss of True Feelings and Purpose

All these losses touch in one way or another on the loss of true feelings and purpose. The farther you get from yourself—through loss of identity, connection, self-worth—the more your individual life comes to lack meaning. Perhaps nothing is more demonstrative of the pain and loss of true feelings and purpose that Powerful Mate Syndrome leaves in its wake than this excerpt from one of my journals.

January 1, 1993 1:41 AM

It is the morning of the first day of the new year. I spent this New Year's Eve doing housework instead of going out by myself as I had planned to hear some good music and enjoy some good food. I thought that perhaps I would get lucky and "S" would go to sleep around 9:30 or 10 PM but I must have been hallucinating. She was up here in my bed driving me crazy with a thousand questions around midnight. It seems that I spend every New Year's Eve doing something other than what I'd like to be doing. About a week ago I was sitting on the floor working on my very late Christmas cards and I found myself wondering if I would be doing the same thing at this time next year . . . feeling as though I have accomplished little or nothing. I must qualify that statement with the fact that giving birth to my second child was the one spectacular event and accomplishment of 1992.

These last couple of weeks have been tiring for me. I can't seem to keep up with the demands of motherhood and everything else I am involved with. I was so fired up about my television project and then had a run-in with James that seemed to just deflate my bubble. I should be immune to him and his comments and actions. God knows that I've lived through enough of them. I don't know what it is about me that allows others to dissuade me so easily. One of the things that I know for sure is that I have to put forth the effort necessary for me to accomplish my goals. I've never been a quitter before in my life. Wait a minute . . . perhaps I have always been a quitter, which would help explain why I have fallen short of so many of my goals in life. I think I just made a great self-discovery just now!

I have been so blessed with material things. I have two lovely children (even though they act so terrible these days) and I have so many opportunities available to me. What is it, I wonder, that keeps me from "going for it" wholeheartedly? I know that I have the intelligence, the wit, etc., the desire, etc. that it takes to make it. Why do I keep holding myself back? I was really angry the other day when someone told me about a "friend" of mine who said that were it not for James, I couldn't make it out here in L.A. and that I should just go back to North Carolina. I'll show her. I don't need "friends" like that and I will be putting some serious distance between her and myself this upcoming year. 1993 is waiting for me and I don't have time to waste on people who don't value me for anything except what I can provide for them materially.

At thirty I am truly at a crossroads in my life. I have two children and I always wanted four. That is until I got a wake-up call and an abrupt lesson in LIFE 101. I no longer love my husband in a way that makes me want to have more children with him. That is so sad and hurtful for me because I truly wanted to have the experience of raising daughters and sons. I also, more than anything else, wanted to always BE in love with James. To realize and truly acknowledge that that part of our relationship is no longer alive is truly a depressing loss for me. It seems that, with the exception of our children and the material things we've acquired, the theme of our marriage is loss. Such a sad commentary on something that started out with such potential and promise. Promise has turned into "com" promise.

—A.

When I wrote that journal entry I was finally at a place where I could at least begin to acknowledge the enormity of loss that I felt in my life. Yet, there are glimmers of hope, indications that all the fire in me hadn't been completely extinguished. Those were my words, my feelings, but I know from the many women with whom I have shared my story (and they theirs, with me) that Powerful Mate Syndrome robs women of their identity, their self-worth, their goals and dreams, the authentic connection to their mate, and their true feelings and purpose for living. Nevertheless, my marriage did not end because of PMS. The moral fiber of it was irreparably damaged. Powerful Mate Syndrome is not a moral issue or problem and no marriage has to end because of it.

My journey toward overcoming my condition was just beginning in 1993. In fact, I remained in that marriage, that house, and in the same bewildering cycle for another year and a half before I could fortify myself sufficiently, mentally and physically, to move in the direction of reclaiming my life. We all get to the work of our lives when the time is right. This is another instance when you cannot use someone else's time frame to work on your life. It is right whenever you decide to get started.

The process of recovering your true feelings and purpose in many ways parallels the recovery of someone battling addiction. You get addicted to feeling empty. You no longer know joy when it is staring you in the face. Numb, stumbling through life as if it were one long, dark hallway is the way life occurs for you when you've hit your "feelings and purpose" bottom. When you come to the point that the feeling that you are most familiar with is feeling sorry for yourself, you've hit bottom. Been there, done that. Done with that forever.

How many of you look for your purpose in the mail-order catalogs that clog your mailbox every day? I tried that route. For a while, I saw my UPS man so many consecutive days that I thought we would end up in the *Guinness Book of World Records* for the greatest number of deliveries in a year. I amassed a lot of stuff, but none of it filled the void. News Flash: Your purpose isn't "out there" somewhere. It isn't for sale. It's within you. It always has been. All you have to do is wake it up.

Think back to what made your heart race when you were eight. What about when you were eighteen? Did the same thing make you weak in the knees when you thought about it at the age of twenty-eight, or had you lost the ability to feel passionate, alive, and pumped up by then?

When I was eight, the thing that made my heart race was getting up in front of people to speak. It didn't matter if I was running for student council or giving a presentation for social studies. I didn't feel like I had butterflies in my stomach when I got ready to go in front of the room, I felt like I had a stomach full of hummingbirds. When I was eighteen, I went to N.C. Girl's State, where I was elected the governor. I thought I had died and gone to heaven. The high I felt back then has been matched only a handful of times since. When I would have to stand up and address my "fellow citizens," I felt a little sick to my stomach, but I also felt so alive, so energized, and so filled with purpose. By the time I was twenty-eight, my feelings about life were on autopilot. I mistakenly thought that my purpose was to be a princess. Translated, that means I thought my purpose was to have as little ambition as possible, to abide by the status quo, and to avoid the despair that was about to crest over my emotional banks, which I dammed up as much as possible.

You can put the book down and go get the Kleenex now if this is your story, too. I know it all too well, and so do many of you who have walked around for years wondering what this cloud was hovering over you. Now you know, and knowledge is the first step in changing anything. You have the choice to do something to banish it from your life. You deserve to have the relationship you want and to feel empowered to make good choices. You are worthy of accomplishing all your dreams, contributing to others, and even to the world if you feel called to do so. You *can* do it. As you will see in the following chapters, if you are willing to give up the fairy-tale beliefs, to make some difficult choices, and to do some hard work, it will be well within your reach. Proceed and Prevail!

PART TWO

THE PMS LESSONS: MY HINDSIGHT AS YOUR FORESIGHT

Living through my experience of Powerful Mate Syndrome would have been an exercise in futility had I decided to keep everything that I learned to myself. Silence does not require courage. It may be safe and secure, but it cannot provide the satisfaction I have felt as a result of sharing what I have learned. That is why I created the next part of this book—The PMS Lessons. Each of the following chapters focuses on a core aspect of Powerful Mate Syndrome that I wish someone had told *me* before I married my "prince" and went off in pursuit of the fairy tale. Whether you are considering marriage or are already married, may they help you cocreate your own long and happy voyage with your very mortal mate.

4

BEGIN WITH THE END IN MIND

> "Love stories always end with the wedding. Maybe that's why there's so much divorce, because there's no role model for how you continue after that new-car smell is gone."
>
> —NOAH HAULEY, *Other People's Weddings*

"BEGIN WITH THE *end* in mind? How unromantic can you get!" That's what I hear from women whenever I broach the subject of this chapter. How can I suggest such a thing? It flies in the face of everything we tell ourselves about marriage and it is completely counter to the romantic mind-set with which most of us approach marriage. But what does that mind-set get us? Fantasies! Fantasies that will, one way or another, be dashed by the realities of married life. Fantasies of happily *ever after*, or, as the character Buzz Lightyear says in the movie *Toy Story*, "To infinity and beyond!"

Listen to me. Your marriage is not a movie, and one day it is going to end. One way or another they all do, and daring to face that inevitability doesn't have to mean taking all the sweetness out of things. It just means going into marriage with your eyes wide open. Now, I'm not saying that divorce is inevitable. Of course it's not. But whether you divorce after a year, your beloved dies in a car crash, or you live together happily until you both reach your nineties, your marriage *is* going to end. That's just a fact.

If each of us went into our relationships fully cognizant of the fact that one day they would end, I believe we would all be much more committed to having the best relationships possible right from the beginning, rather than waiting to look back on them once they were irretrievably lost or damaged beyond repair. If we were truly present to the fact that we only have a finite amount of time with the person we deeply love, we would be less likely to take him or her for granted, to break our promises to that person, and more likely to appreciate and celebrate every moment we are given with them. When we are aware of the ending of things right from the beginning, we savor what's in between so much more. The whole point of the beginning and the end is really about the middle! It is about being in the here and now; here and now because you know that the end *will* come—some time, some way. Maybe sooner, maybe later, but it will come.

Think of all the husbands and wives who, on the morning of September 11, 2001, simply assumed that their beloveds would be coming home later that evening. When those jets flew into the Twin Towers and the Pentagon and that fourth plane crashed into a field in Pennsylvania, the spouses of everyone who died experienced an ending on that day. Let's just hope that many of them had an end in mind and didn't take their days together for granted. Certainly no one could have predicted those particular endings. All the more reason to begin with the end in mind. When we assume we have forever to "get it right," we miss an awful lot of opportunities to make it right *now*. We miss out on all the love we could experience with each other right now.

The only place where love is forever is in fairy tales.

Why are we so afraid to embrace the fact of the end? Why does it usually take a catastrophe, either physical or psychological, to make us begin behaving as though time or our relationship is valuable? Perhaps it is simply because we are human, but that's always a convenient excuse to justify putting forth less effort than is needed. I think we do it because it's just plain *easier* to see marriage through the fairy-tale lens than the realistic one. When we put on our realistic glasses, we see that marriage and relationships:

- are not warm and fuzzy all the time

- require hard work and dedication

- are unpredictable

- don't always end with happily ever after

But those very same realistic lenses can also give a glimpse of the possibilities that marriage and a good relationship can bring. *Realistically*, marriages can:

- be incredibly rewarding and meaningful

- take the meaning of love and ecstasy to new heights

- expand one's life in unimaginable ways

We have to ask ourselves: If we are so averse to looking down the road, why do we continue to embark upon the journey in the first place?

Two years ago, I took a cross-country road trip from California to North Carolina with my mother and two daughters. Weeks before our departure date, I went to the Automobile Club and got every map and hotel guide that we might possibly need. I mapped out the entire trip, complete with every hotel we would stop at and the number of miles I would drive each day. I had the minivan serviced and made arrangements for someone to stay in my home with the dog while we were gone. I left no stone unturned, and you know what? It was one of the most wonderful vacations I have ever had. Why? Because I asked myself from the moment that I thought about making the trip, "How do I want all of us to feel about this trip when it's all over?" I began with the end in mind and was able to plan the trip in a way that would help all of us feel that it was a great and valuable adventure.

If we look at marriage as a road trip, knowing full well from the outset that before we reach our destination we will encounter all types of challenges, then we can prepare to meet and overcome those challenges using the gift of foresight—and then relax into the adventure.

Yes, of course, you can't really compare a road trip and a marriage, but isn't it just a little ironic that we will spend so much time planning and thinking about a vacation, but put blinders on when it comes to thinking ahead about marriage?

It's my guess that we don't ask ourselves questions like, "How do I want to think back on this journey twenty or thirty years from now?" or "What lasting memories do I hope to create?" because then we'd have to be *accountable* for the way things unfold in our marriages, and most of us don't have the courage to do that. Yes, that is harsh talk, but it's true. Consider it Angela's tough love.

I'm asking you to consider the *possibility* in those questions. Imagine how awesome our marriages could be if we were willing to get real and make some plans. I want you to delete the idea that marriage is some kind of fantasy and begin yours (or rethink it) with your mind on the end: a *happy* ending. You can have that happy ending if you and your mate are willing to create it together, if you are willing to begin with the end in mind.

Women married to powerful mates have a particular challenge in this regard, especially those married to men of wealth and fame. Why? Because both can be so fleeting. If you are married to a wealthy or famous man, I want you to take a few moments to ask yourself the following questions:

- If all this wealth evaporated tomorrow, what would it mean to my self-worth and the way I feel about myself?

- If this wealth disappeared tomorrow, would my relationship be the same as it is today?

- How much of my commitment to this relationship is influenced by my partner's wealth or fame?

- What will I do when this fame or wealth is no longer here?

- Will my relationship end when the fame or money ends?

These may sound like questions that only a very shallow person would ask, but I just want you to consider what would happen to your relationship if its initial terms changed. It happens all the time. We enter into a relationship under one set of circumstances but then things change. Sometimes, of course, the change is for the better. You have great success, bring children into your lives, etc. But reversals happen, too, and rarely does the end of a career, a loss of income, or a loss of status *not* affect a relationship. It's never too soon to ask yourself,

- Am I really in this relationship for richer or poorer?

- If my mate were downsized from his six- or seven-figure job, how would I react?

- If my spouse were tried and convicted of embezzlement of funds, what would I do?

- If I were no longer able to drive my swanky European luxury car that cost the same as the gross national product of a small nation, how would I handle it?

In the early years of my marriage to James I never seriously took the time to consider what life would be like for us after his playing days were over. It never occurred to me that life would be anything other than what I had imagined in my fairy-tale, fantasy-contaminated mind. I never noticed then, certainly not the way I do now, how often marriages of professional athletes fall apart shortly after their careers are over. I'm sure this is just as true in the business world. It's not all about the money. It's not just that the gravy train (the large salary) stops. Rather, it's that suddenly the man has to concentrate on his marriage. As long as he's involved in sports (or building and running the company), everyone expects him to put all his physical and psychological energy into the game (business). Most wives understand this because they too live, eat, and sleep the sport. But once he retires he is faced with the reality of how much hard work having a good marriage is; the reality that marriage is often more difficult to deal with than a hundred-game season. And she is faced with the reality that the thing that she thought kept them *apart* for all this time (his sport/profession) was actually the thing that kept them *together*. When that's gone, then what? These are questions that couples would be better off posing, even if they cannot answer them, at the beginning of their life together, rather than waiting for the moment when the questions come raining down on their heads.

You've probably heard the saying: "No one lying on their death bed says, 'I wish I had worked more.'" Maybe not, but I bet a lot of people would like to say: *I wish I had . . .*

- . . . made amends with my spouse while I was able to do so

- . . . apologized to my friend whom I offended or betrayed

- . . . stopped drinking so much—maybe I wouldn't be hoping for a liver transplant and my wife wouldn't be going through this agony with me

- . . . written a will when I was in control of my mental faculties

- . . . purchased some life insurance so my family could at least bury me without it causing a hardship

- . . . given more of what I had to those less fortunate

- . . . given more of my time instead of just writing a check

As you know, I learned all this the hard way, but you don't have to: Beginning with the end in mind just means being *proactive* when it comes to your relationship. And being proactive means dealing with things that we usually consider unpleasant. Attending to the following list of things forces you to acknowledge that you are mortal, not a prince or princess who will live eternally. It all comes full circle in the discussion about Powerful Mate Syndrome, because when you live in the fairy tale, none of these things are relevant, but as soon as you close the book on the fairy tale, you have to deal with the fact that there is no "happily ever after." Better sooner rather than later. Do you have:

Funds reserved for retirement?	Health Insurance?
Life Insurance?	A Last Will and Testament?
A Revocable Trust?	Peace of Mind?

Cinderella and her prince never had to worry about their ending because they didn't live in the real world. You don't live in their world and you simply cannot afford to act as if you do. The stakes are too high and the cost to your happiness and well-being will be greater than you ever imagined. Start thinking about the end—before it's too late!

If you need guidance on how and where to start, try going to one of my favorite places—the public library. Go to the reference desk and tell the librarian what kind of information you are seeking. A whole new world and the opportunity to radically shape the nature of your life from this point on await you! Proceed and Prevail!

5

INVEST IN COUPLES COUNSELING

"Though marriage makes man and wife one flesh, it leaves 'em still two fools."

—WILLIAM CONGREVE

POWERFUL MATE SYNDROME can only exist in the mind of a woman who is under the influence of the "Powerful Prince" fantasy. It simply cannot take root and survive in the mind of a woman who has realistic expectations about her relationship and a clear understanding of herself and her mate. That's why it is so important to invest in counseling. There is something of value for nearly every couple at any stage of their relationship. Whether you are newly engaged, newly married, been married for several years, or in a committed dating situation is irrelevant. Of all the PMS lessons, this one can have the single largest impact on whether or not you succumb to Powerful Mate Syndrome: Get some counseling, *especially* if you think you are marrying your prince.

That advice especially applies to those of you who are already married to your prince but who find yourselves wondering whether or not he's a toad at times. You probably got married with less preparation and knowledge about marriage and your spouse than I would suggest is preferable.

But it is never too late to take steps to improve your communication, deepen your understanding of yourself and your mate, and increase the overall satisfaction with your marriage. Counseling done with a good practitioner, especially when both parties are committed to a great outcome, is always a good thing. I believe that every couple should do marriage maintenance work, whether it is seeing a counselor every so often, taking weekend trips devoted to working on the relationship, or attending a retreat for couples annually. We change the oil in our cars every three thousand miles. Consider what a difference it would make in our relationships if every time we changed our car's oil, we sat down and had a heart-to-heart talk with our partner about the state of our marriage. We would probably need less divorce lawyers!

Daniel and David have been a couple for eight and a half years. They met shortly after Daniel broke off another long-term relationship with a man named Wayne. Even though the relationship was over, many of Wayne's possessions as well as a large framed picture of him remained in Daniel's condominium. At first it wasn't a big issue. However, as their relationship became more serious and David moved into the condo, he began to feel threatened and annoyed that Daniel had not removed Wayne's things. Their conversations about the situation began to turn into shouting matches, which led to very hurt feelings for both men. Finally, on the recommendation of a close friend, Daniel and David found a counselor and began to deal with the situation.

In a relatively short time they were able to reach a mutually satisfying resolution of their problem. As a result of their positive experiences in counseling, Daniel and David decided that they would go to counseling for a relationship tune-up on a regular basis. They don't wait for years and let small issues grow into large ones. Their system is based on the seasons. Four times a year they go to eight hours of counseling. On four consecutive weeks they will attend a two-hour session with their therapist. That amounts to thirty-two hours a year. When you think about it, that is less time than most people spend working each *week*.

Daniel and David believe that spending time exploring their relationship in a safe and supportive environment has enabled it to thrive, while many of their friends who don't invest in counseling are struggling to keep their relationships together.

I had neither realistic expectations nor a clear understanding of marriage when I entered it. All I brought to the table were youth, ignorance, and, truthfully, a great deal of arrogance. Arrogance in the sense that I thought I knew everything there was to know about myself and what kind of marriage I wanted. It turns out that I *did* know what kind of marriage I wanted. I just didn't know what it would take to have it.

It was very easy for me to fall in love with James. He had a gentle, endearing manner that balanced his imposing physical presence. He was no saint, but he had not yet been exposed to all the "goodies" that come along with being a celebrity athlete. When we met, he was still more of a "good ole boy" than a playboy. It was very easy to plug him into my fantasy of the prince who would come to my rescue. He was already larger than life and had an aura of power surrounding him. I'm sure he had no idea of the burden I was pinning on him psychologically. I would go so far as to say that it's unfair and unreasonable to do this to any man, but that's just what we women who sculpt our dreams out of fairy tales do. Premarital counseling could have helped me get my head out of the fairy tale and into reality.

James and I dated for three years prior to our marriage, but I didn't really know him. Subconsciously I didn't really *want* to know him, because that might have ruined my fantasy that he was infallible. Had I made the effort to understand him, myself, and the dynamics of our relationship, then I would not have been able to feign ignorance when it all began to unravel. Better still, we might have been able to foresee the unraveling and deal with our problems up front!

At the time that I got married, I didn't understand how valuable counseling could be. Like a lot of people, I believed that counseling was for people "with problems." I didn't realize that getting some counseling is actually a way of showing one's commitment to the relationship and future spouse. We need to discard any remaining stigma attached to counseling. I spent ten months planning our wedding. By contrast, we didn't spend ten hours planning our marriage. We left everything to chance, which is the equivalent of playing Russian roulette. Sooner or later, someone is going to get hurt. I had such a high stake in keeping myself in denial that I swaddled myself in a blanket of delusion. I told myself that I was indeed the embodiment of Cinderella and I was going to have my fairy-tale life—no matter what the cost! Not to mention that I had all the dreams and hopes of my family and friends riding on this gigantic fantasy world that I had created in my mind.

Let's face it. "Love conquers all" is a myth. Instead of facing the reality of our less than perfect relationship, I told myself that I could learn to live with the things about our relationship that caused me anxiety. But nothing ever changes or goes away because you deny its existence. Not ever. The temporary solution for not dealing with reality was that I became a master at "productive avoidance." That simply means I did everything that I could to avoid confronting reality.

I meticulously planned the wedding; I shopped excessively; I went to lunch with every old friend from home who I hadn't seen since I went off to college. In a nutshell, I did everything but stop and face the fact that we had issues that were only going to get bigger after we were married if we didn't face them before. Neither of us knew how to deal with confrontation very well, so avoiding difficult issues in our relationship became a way of life for James and me. Be forewarned: *Avoidance is a very dangerous game.* No ceremony, no matter how grand, is going to make the core issues in your relationship disappear. And believe me, no fairy godmother with a magic wand can make them disappear either. If I could dispense one piece of advice it would be to *spend less money on your wedding and more time in counseling.*

With a commitment as serious as marriage, it behooves you to take every step that will help you enter it with the greatest chance of success. Marriage is, in many ways, like any other contract that you enter into. Ignorance is no excuse; you have to read the fine print. In marriage, the "fine print" is all those little things you've been ignoring but really have a problem with deep down. It's your family history and your partner's family history. It's all that baggage that you drag into your new relationship from all your past ones. It's the fantasy and the delusions that you cling to, despite the warning signs, about your partner being your "prince."

Just as in medicine, in relationships, early detection is a

lifesaver. Many of the most difficult problems people face in their marriages actually surface long before the wedding day. We ignore them at our peril.

Even if everything seems to be going "fine," marriage means pledging a lifelong commitment to another person. Doesn't it only seem right that you would spend some time dealing with any doubts and concerns either of you have, or exposing some of your expectations about marriage to a little scrutiny? It doesn't matter what you do for a living, whether you live in a sprawling estate or a modest apartment, drive a Mercedes or a Ford, are Christian, Muslim, or Jewish. No one gets married in a vacuum. Even if you feel that you have no skeletons in your closet (and really now, who doesn't?), when you marry your "prince," you are also marrying every one of his past experiences, the people in his family, and his beliefs and values, whether you share them or not. If you think that his father walking out on his mother when he was eleven years old won't have an effect on your marriage, you are living in a fairy tale. If you believe that your prince will stop smoking pot after you exchange wedding vows just because he says he will, even though he's been smoking it since he was in grade school, you're under the influence of a fantasy. You can tell yourself that he's going to stop going to the local strip club after your wedding day because it's too painful to think of him doing otherwise, but sweetheart, you are caught in the dream. It is time to wake up. Stop hitting the snooze button and face reality.

Most of us are so caught up in the "fun" parts of being with our partner that we neglect looking at the less attractive underbelly of the relationship. We are like the little child who thinks there's a monster under the bed but isn't courageous enough to look under it alone. The child needs his parent and perhaps a flashlight to confront whatever it is under the bed. You and your partner need a qualified counselor to help you shine a light on whatever it is that you have been avoiding "under the bed" of your relationship.

Speaking of beds, please, please listen to me when I say, *Don't mistake good sex for good communication!* It's too easy to do, especially in the early years of a relationship. Of course, there's absolutely nothing wrong with great sex; it just isn't a substitute for communicating effectively with each other. That's a skill at which it takes time and prolonged effort to become proficient. Any relationship in which the partners are lousy communicators eventually ends up being a lousy relationship. You both have to commit to keeping the lines of communication open, and that's where counseling can really help.

Before you begin your search for a counselor, you and your mate will need to decide on a couple of things, such as:

- *Does either of you have a preference about the gender of the counselor?* For some people, the counselor's gender is irrelevant. For others, it is very important. For example, you never want your mate to feel as though he or she is being ganged up on or tag-teamed. This is a common fear men have when the counselor is female. However, a good counselor will be cognizant of that issue and will be fair and show no favoritism towards either of you.

- *Is there a dollar amount for the counselor's services that you feel comfortable spending?* Fees can vary widely depending on the counselor's level of experience, education, and location. You should discuss this before you embark on your search. Keep in mind, though, that the amount of a counselor's fee should not lead you to reject one that you like outright. Sometimes a counselor or therapist will work on a sliding scale that will take into consideration your ability to pay based on your level of income.

Another thing to keep in mind is that the size of a fee is not an indicator of suitability or skill to deal with your particular issues. I was a client of a very famous Ph.D. who has published books and is widely renowned in psychology circles. His fee reflected his fame, but the results we achieved in my brief work with him were far less satisfactory and useful than those that I got with another therapist whose fee was half of his. You might also find that working with a registered marriage and family therapy intern meets your needs. An intern has completed the training and education required by law and is permitted to see clients under the close supervision of a licensed Marriage Family Therapist or psychologist (Ph.D.).

Selecting a counselor or therapist can be similar to the process of buying a car. You begin with an idea of what it is that you desire and then you go to the dealership to test-drive your top candidates. Unlike car shopping, however, you don't have to deal with the heavy sales pitch. Eventually you go with the one that best suits your needs.

Your search may differ depending on where you live. For example, if you live in a large urban area, you might find that people are pretty uninhibited when it comes to talking about their therapist. They'll recommend their therapist to you as easily as they will recommend a good restaurant.

There just isn't the same stigma that you can find in smaller communities.

That said, some people will feel uncomfortable sharing their most intimate information with a counselor or therapist whom their best friend also sees. It might be too close for comfort for you. You should know that no practitioner worth his or her salt is ever going to discuss your business with another client or another client's business with you. That isn't ethical. But you will have to decide whether you'd be comfortable seeing a friend's therapist or even asking a friend for a recommendation.

Sometimes there are cultural barriers to seeking counseling. During my youth I would sometimes hear people say, "Counseling is for crazy people." Or sometimes people would say that counseling was just a way to avoid taking responsibility for one's actions. Those are two misconceptions that still persist in some cultures. If you are hesitant to seek counseling because of what family members or friends might think, don't tell them about it. When they begin to see the positive changes in your relationship they will most likely inquire about what is going on. Should you choose to do so, that might be the perfect opportunity to share your new secret weapon with them. It is completely up to you whether or not you share your business with anyone, but there is certainly nothing about seeking counseling that should make you feel ashamed or embarrassed. It is something to bring to the attention of your therapist or counselor if it is a concern of yours.

What should you expect from counseling? That is like asking what to expect from childbirth: Each person will have a different experience. Even the two individuals in a couple will have varying perceptions, because what we experience is always partly determined by our experiences in our family of origin, in past relationships, and by a variety of factors we bring to the current relationship. What you *can* expect is that you will learn more about yourself and your mate than you knew before you began the process. With any luck you will learn new communication skills or sharpen those that are already working for you. Perhaps the best thing that I can say about expectation is paradoxical. On the one hand, expectation often leads to upset and disappointment. On the other hand, I always tell expectant mothers to expect the best of their experience. Therefore, expect nothing and expect the best!

Your family doctor is always a good place to ask for a referral to a therapist. Another place to seek information is your health insurance company. Even if you don't plan to use your health insurance to pay for the services, you can always inquire about a referral. In this age, when it seems that talking to a human being requires an act of Congress, you can probably bypass speaking to someone and go directly to your health insurance company's Web site. It's just another possible option available to you.

Your local college or university may have counseling services available as well. They might even have a dedicated counseling center, such as the one that existed at Antioch University, where I earned my master's degree in clinical psychology. Often the professors are practicing therapists and psychologist and see clients that come into the counseling center. In such a setting, there is also the likelihood of being able to pay according to a sliding scale.

The mental health department of your local city or county

government is another valuable resource. Often counseling is offered by hospitals as well.

Every state has an agency that governs the ethics, licensing, and general business practices of mental health practitioners. In California, it is the Board of Behavioral Sciences. You can always call the state agency for guidance if none of the other recommendations are fruitful. Most states also have associations made up of mental health practitioners. In California it is called CAMFT—California Association of Marriage and Family Therapists. Check your local telephone directory for a similar association in the state where you live. Call and ask about anything that you would like to know more about. Knowledge is power and sometimes all it takes is a question to unlock it.

We often overlook the telephone book as a resource now that we have the Internet, but it can also be useful in locating various mental health services. I don't recommend choosing a counselor randomly from the book, but you can get an idea of the availability of counseling resources.

The Internet can be a wonderful place to acquire information, but it is also a place that affords those with questionable motivations license to operate in obscurity and virtual anonymity. I do not recommend choosing a counselor based on something you see on the Internet unless you can verify his or her credentials. Finding the right person to work with is too important to leave solely to an Internet search.

No matter where you eventually find the counselor that is right for you, check her or his credentials. Your state licensing board can help you with that information, should you need help in doing so.

<u>Six Scenarios: Cautionary Tales</u>

James and I always had numerous distractions that enabled us to "productively avoid" taking an honest look at our relationship. Like so many brides, I simply convinced myself that things would be different after we took our marriage vows. For all the following couples, the handwriting was on the wall long before the marriage; they just chose not to see it.

Scenario A

Sabrina had a joint credit card account with her fiancé Isaac. One day, she opened the monthly statement and noticed a sizeable charge from a women's lingerie store in a city where Isaac had traveled for a business trip the previous month. It was definitely his signature on the photocopy of the receipt that came along with the statement. It had been her birthday the week before, but she hadn't received lingerie from Isaac, and they didn't have an anniversary or special occasion coming up. That night at dinner she asked him about it. Instead of giving Sabrina a direct answer, Isaac responded, "I don't have the slightest idea what you're talking about; there must be some mistake." He hung her out to dry like the laundry. Sabrina decided not to pursue it further, even though she knew there was no "mistake." That was the end of the conversation, but it was hardly the end of her feelings about the situation. Although she was left feeling dismissed and confused, she was more concerned that Isaac might think she was questioning his integrity than she was about her own feelings and needs.

Scenario B

Haley's future in-laws invited her to Sunday dinner at their home. Her fiancé, Brandon, has six siblings—three sisters and three brothers. Everything went smoothly during dinner, but afterwards Brandon and his siblings decided to go out to the garage to "catch up" with each other. They left Haley to play Scrabble with his parents. After playing a couple of games with them, Haley excused herself to go join the "garage gang." She walked into a cloud of marijuana smoke so thick she could have cut it with a knife. In the middle of the room was a makeshift table. On it was a heaping pile of white powder. Although Haley had never experimented with cocaine, she knew that it was not confectioner's sugar. Without saying a word to Brandon, she bolted from the garage and spent the remainder of the evening watching television and chatting with his parents. Brandon's parents were totally clueless that they were hosting a cocaine convention in their garage.

Later that night, Haley asked Brandon about what she had witnessed earlier. He brushed it off as "something we do whenever we get together." He promised her that once they were married he would walk away from it forever. Because she adored him and wanted so badly for this to be true, Haley accepted his word and dropped the subject. Even though she had very strong feelings against drug use, even if it was just recreational, Haley didn't want to risk "rocking the boat." She told herself that it was "Brandon's family problem" and that it would stop after they were married.

Scenario C

Catherine loved to read and would often climb into bed with a stack of books. She kept a dictionary on her nightstand at all times in case she came across a word that she didn't know in her reading material. When her fiancé Chris climbed into bed one night he gave her a look of disbelief. (She was supposed to be able to read his mind and know that he's feeling amorous.) He said to Catherine, "It's bad enough that I have to compete with reruns of *Friends*, but I also have to scale the 'Great Wall of Books' to get close to you. Damn, what does a man have to do to get some affection around here?" Chris stormed out of the room, put on a sweat suit, grabbed his keys, and left the house. He didn't even take his cell phone.

At four AM Catherine heard him return, but he didn't come up to their bedroom. He slept on the sofa in the den. In the morning, he acted as if nothing happened. Chris didn't offer Catherine any explanation for his behavior, much less an apology. Catherine simply chalked it up to "a bad night."

Scenario D

Petra and her fiancé Pierre went to a popular nightclub to do some dancing. In the club was a man with whom Petra had had a brief but torrid relationship before she met Pierre. During the course of the evening, Petra had one dance with him. She spent the rest of the evening focused entirely on Pierre. Later that night, the other man sent a bottle of

Petra's favorite champagne over to their table. This infuriated Pierre. Petra immediately suggested that they go home because she wanted to avoid a potential confrontation between her fiancé and her former boyfriend. There was complete silence in the car all the way home. As soon as they got into the house, Pierre slapped her so hard that she not only saw stars but the entire galaxy. No man had ever hit her before. At that moment Petra said she remembered that her mother used to say, "If a man hits you once, shame on him. If he hits you twice, shame on you!" Petra's first instinct was to pack a bag and get the hell out of there, but instead, she picked herself up, took a cold shower to stop the burning feeling on the side of her face, crawled into bed, and cried herself to sleep.

Pierre apologized profusely the next morning, but not without insinuating that the blame was hers. He promised Petra he would not lose control of himself again, so she didn't tell a soul about it. She prayed that it would never happen again.

Scenario E

Margo had a very successful career as a veterinarian and ran her own animal hospital. Even though Howie's income was enough to provide them both with a very lavish lifestyle, it was always her intention to continue working after they married. Her work meant more to her than just a way to make money. It gave her a great sense of accomplishment and allowed her to express her love for animals. One day, Margo and Howie were having a fabulous lunch in her favorite restaurant when he dropped the bomb that he expected her to stop working once they were married. He told her that he wanted them to start their family right away. Margo nearly choked on her seared tuna. She was perplexed as to why he would think that a career woman like herself would be in agreement with such an old-fashioned idea. Rather than speak up and tell him that her intentions didn't include having children at all, she just laughed it off and continued her meal. Margo didn't bother to tell him that she had given birth to a child during her sophomore year in college and had not only put it up for adoption, but had gotten a tubal ligation. She changed the subject as quickly as she could and decided it was better not to discuss it any further until after their wedding.

Scenario F

Tess and Dominick went away for a long weekend at a five-star spa and resort. She wanted to eat, sleep, and frequent the spa as much as possible during their stay. Dominick, an avid golfer, wanted to play thirty-six holes of golf every day.

Everything was going smoothly until Dominick returned from his golf game on Saturday night, sunburned and with a twisted lower back. All he wanted was room service, a shower, and to go to bed. Tess, on the other hand, was feeling rested and ready for an evening of robust, athletic sex. She attempted to rouse Dominick's interest with sexy lingerie, champagne, and romantic music, but Dominick was totally wiped out, and he couldn't have faked interest even if he had wanted to. Tess wouldn't quit, and eventually Dominick became annoyed, snapping at her, "Maybe you need to find yourself someone who's more sexually compatible with you!" Needless to say, that completely ruined Tess's hopes for a sexual liaison that night.

Dominick hit the shower and Tess took her knitting out of her bag and finished the sweater she was making for her miniature poodle, Sasha. Tess assumed that Dominick was only joking, even though she noticed that she was always more interested in sex than he was. She told herself that this "problem" would go away as soon as they were married.

No One's Perfect

All of these couples needed counseling—badly. If you and your mate have never dealt with a situation similar to theirs, congratulations. You may count yourselves among a rare minority (though I would bet you've had concerns or issues I may not have covered). The reality for the remaining ninety-nine percent of us is that we have either lived through one or more of those scenarios or we know someone who has. Some of you will follow your first inclination, which may be to dismiss whatever has happened in the past because, after all, "it's over." However, we human beings are complex, and the ironic thing about the past is that unless you take the necessary actions to put it in its place, it just keeps showing up.

One of the keys to preventing Powerful Mate Syndrome lies in identifying and isolating those beliefs and behaviors that do not empower you *before* you take them into your marriage. Here is another parallel with the sports world: *A good defense is a good offense.* If you defend your relationship from these types of beliefs and behaviors from the outset, you greatly diminish the likelihood that you will succumb to Powerful Mate Syndrome. This sounds simple, but it isn't. Unless you are both a highly skilled communicator and very good listener, identifying the beliefs and behaviors can end up being a hornet's nest. That is why I strongly suggest that you bring in an experienced, neutral third party. The statements at the end of the chapter might stimulate you to think about this in a way you never have. We are so used to assuming that we know our own beliefs and behaviors that we sometimes don't become aware of them until they are made conscious, specific, and even spoken out loud. You may be surprised at some of your own feelings. On some of them you and your mate might agree, on others you might strongly disagree, and on some you may just agree to disagree. Wherever the results lie, it is far better to get as much as possible out in the open before you commit yourself to a relationship for the rest of your life.

I haven't forgotten about those of you who are already married or in long-term, committed relationships. Many of your issues as a couple are probably already apparent, so in a sense you can hit the ground running in counseling. You've been living with your partner for some time and you've probably identified the areas that need the attention. You should follow the exact same steps that a couple seeking premarital counseling would in terms of your search for a counselor. After you find the one that you both agree on, there is nothing left but to pick up the telephone along with your calendar and make that first appointment.

Couples counseling is one of the best defenses you can avail yourselves of. It will help you and your mate to leave the fairy-tale behind and see marriage and each other in realistic terms. If you are considering marriage, the worst that can happen is that you'll find out that your relationship is not based on anything worth pursuing and you will call the whole thing off, but at least you will have the opportunity to avert the disaster before it occurs. Believe me, it will be far worse to find out *after* you're married.

If you are already married you will probably discover issues that will fall into one (but possibly more) of the following categories.

- Things that you don't like in your relationship but believe can be dealt with to your mutual satisfaction.

- Things that you don't like that may require compromise on both your parts.

- Things that you absolutely cannot live with and will not compromise on.

- Things that you discover you are happy about in your relationship and want to build upon.

Going to couples counseling when you are already married is just as revealing as it is for those still in the wedding-planning stage. If you find that you need to end your relationship, then so be it. Sure, it will be difficult to end things, but once you get over the initial disappointment and hurt you'll be forever grateful that you didn't put or keep yourself in a marriage that was destined to fail. Proceed and Prevail!

Marriage Deal Breakers That Counseling Can Bring to Light

The following are just some of the beliefs and behaviors that couples often sweep under the rug even though they are potential "deal breakers" in a marriage. I encourage you to explore issues like these together, ideally *before* you get married. However, all is not lost if you're already married. This is a worthwhile exercise at any point in a relationship, and the time you invest doing so will pay huge dividends whether you are newly engaged or about to celebrate your tenth anniversary. Saying wedding vows does not automatically absolve you and your partner from ever having to deal with difficult issues. And it certainly doesn't mean that you'll be in agreement about everything! That is all the more reason to purposefully discuss your differences before they become irreconcilable.

- She believes that a married woman should be able to stay at home and make it an inviting place for her husband to come home to after a hard day's work.

  He believes that a married woman should make the home an inviting place to come home to for her husband, as soon as she gets home from working at her paying job.

- He believes that a man should not have to give up his weekend basketball games with his buddies at the local park after he's married.

  She believes that a man should reserve his weekends for family time, not hanging out and playing "silly" games with his friends.

- She believes that a woman should not have children until after she has accomplished her career goals.

  He believes that if he's not going to be a father, there is no point in being married.

- She believes that it is important to have the latest, fastest luxury SUV to drive, even if it means losing money to upgrade each year.

  He believes that investing in a home is more important than providing a new luxury SUV for his wife every year.

- He believes that husbands and wives should take vacations without other family members or friends tagging along.

  She believes that husbands and wives should bring members of their extended families along on their vacations.

- She believes that there is nothing wrong with creating her own adult entertainment Web site as a means of making extra income.

  He is repulsed by adult entertainment in any form.

- She believes that a man should never receive spousal support in a divorce.

  He believes that a spouse should get spousal support if he or she is entitled to it under the law and wants it.

- He believes that it is okay to "knock a little sense" into a woman every now and then.

  She believes that there is no such thing as degrees of abusiveness and therefore it is permissible to use deadly force against an abusive spouse under any circumstances.

- He believes that adultery should be a three-strikes-and-you're-out offense.

  She believes that adultery is forgivable once but doesn't believe in multiple offenses.

- She believes that the responsibility for birth control belongs to the man since he doesn't have to deal with being pregnant.

  He believes that birth control is the woman's responsibility.

- He believes that a man's home is his temple and should be respected as such.

  She believes that she should be able to smoke marijuana in the privacy of their home, even if he disapproves of it.

- He believes that it is important that she convert to his religion.

  She is agnostic and believes that he should abandon religion in all forms.

- He believes there is nothing wrong with consuming alcohol while driving as long as he can still see the road markings.

  She thinks it is never okay to drink and drive.

- She thinks that it is really cool to keep loaded guns in the house.

  He thinks a gun, unloaded and locked up, in the house is tolerable.

- He believes that his wife becomes his "possession" once he gets married.

She could not fathom ever thinking of herself as someone's possession.

- She wants her to wear provocative, revealing clothing when she's out in public with her husband so everyone can see how lucky he is.

  He believes that his wife should dress conservatively when they are out in public.

6

CREATE YOUR GAME PLAN

**"Power comes from living in the present moment,
where you can take action and create the future."**

—SANAYA ROMAN

SPORTS OFFER lots of useful analogies for our intimate relationships. One of the things that became a fixture in our household during the years that James played professional basketball was a playbook. His playbook ranked second in importance behind the Bible. It was thick and heavy: filled to capacity with page after page of diagrams detailing the team's offensive and defensive schemes. The coaches would formulate a plan of attack for every game, and every conceivable play that they might run was contained in that book. The game plan, therefore, was a plan for victory. No coach worth his or her salt goes into a game without a plan and an enormous amount of preparation. That is one practice in sports that we would be smart to apply to marriage.

Your game plan for marriage is one way to concretize the fact that it is not a fairy tale. The adage, "A failure to plan is a plan for failure," is never more true than when it is used with marriage in mind.

Those of you who want to treat marriage as if it is a fairy

tale and believe that everything will somehow magically work itself out are still stuck in the land of pixie dust, magic red slippers, and pumpkins that turn into carriages. The rest of you, get ready to create a game plan that will form the foundation of a reality tale that is capable of bringing you the joy and satisfaction you desire in your relationship and in your life. If the sports analogy doesn't resonate with you, look at it this way: Your marriage is like a house that you are building from the ground up. When an architect creates a blueprint for a house, no detail is overlooked. Nothing is left to chance, and the result is an edifice that functions well, looks beautiful, and hopefully exceeds the expectations of those who will dwell in it. They don't have to worry about whether the wiring plan was correct, if the toilets are in the bathrooms, or whether the gas dryer is vented to the outdoors. All they have to do is inhabit it. Don't you want to be able to inhabit a comfortable marriage that exceeds your expectations?

Bear in mind that, unlike your prenuptial agreement, which we'll get to in the next chapter, this game plan is not a legally binding document. The only thing that binds you to this is your commitment to your partner and your relationship. The greatest requirement in this endeavor is your integrity. James and I never had a game plan, although now I could not fathom being in a relationship that was important to me and not having one. It will give you incredible insight into yourself and your partner and you will probably learn things about both of you that you had never thought about before. If you do this openly and honestly, I can guarantee that you will deepen your connection with your partner.

Convinced? Then let's get started.

Getting Started on Your Game Plan

1. **Begin working on your game plan as soon as you begin seriously to consider marriage.** Most people have some time between their engagement and the day they actually get married. Use it wisely. James and I were engaged nearly a year before we were married. Time was not the issue. I was just so arrogant that I didn't believe that there was anything I didn't know about James, myself, or marriage. And James, well, I think he was relying on the *prayer* method—you just *pray* that everything works out! Even if you're already married, working on a game plan is an excellent way to focus and strengthen your relationship. It is never too late to embark on a plan to improve your relationship.

2. **Leave no stone unturned.** Your game plan is all about foreseeing what issues might become problems in your marriage. The best thing you can do is leave no stone unturned. In other words, here's your chance to explore all the issues, or at least the ones you are aware of, that you will have to deal with in your relationship. This is not the time for holding back. Every concern, question, and issue is fair game. If you want to know how your partner's parents dealt with finances and how your mate expects to do so, bring it up. If you haven't told your fiancé that you were sexually abused as a child by your father's best friend, now's the time to do so. If you think your husband may want you to quit your job when you start having kids, ask him now to discuss it with you. If you have avoided certain issues because you were afraid

of your partner's reaction, now is the time to summon the courage to bring them up. Why would you want to wait until after you're married to deal with it? Marriage vows are not some magic wand that can make anything unpleasant in your relationship just disappear. Believe me, I tried going that route and it's only a dead end. When you turn yourself around to go in the opposite direction, that same issue that you tried to avoid is right there staring you in the eye.

3. **Work on the game plan together.** It's extremely important that this be a *joint* project. After all, you're both getting married, right? If you meet resistance, consider that a trouble sign for the relationship. If you're one of those people who feels lonely even when you're with your partner, you might want to take a look at that and see what it means. Maybe you don't have the connection that you think you do and you are expecting marriage to "fix it." Well, it won't, and you'll be doing yourself a favor to think about that dynamic more deeply before you say "I do."

4. **It doesn't matter how you package it.** Whether you house your game plan in a beautiful blank book from the art store or simply jot some things down in a spiral notebook makes no difference. My personal recommendation is to use a three-ring view binder with several sections—the kind into which you can insert your own cover. That way you can have an 8×10 photo of the two of you on the front. I always think it's helpful to use a photo that shows the two of you really enjoying each

other's company, something that captures the spirit or essence of the relationship. That way you have a visual to refer back to when things get rough.

If you go the binder route, you can label a section divider for every issue that comes to mind. You might have as few as five or as many as twenty. It is limited only by your life together and your imagination. There are no right or wrong issues. The only valid criterion here is that these be issues of concern to one or both of you.

5. **How much time you spend on your game plan is up to you.** My only piece of advice here would be not to spend so much time on it that it becomes a chore. Some couples choose to go away for an entire weekend and devote themselves to working on it. These are people who can stand being immersed in something for long periods of time. I tend to be that type of person. Others choose to work on it for twenty minutes once a week and that works just fine for them. This is not a one-size-fits-all kind of endeavor.

6. **Remember that this is a valuable keepsake, not a weapon.** If you want to be really thorough you can write down your responses to each issue and keep them in your book. Or you can simply write down the question or issue and just discuss it. Because I keep a journal and love putting things on paper, I would write down everything. That also gives you something tangible to refer back to if you want to refresh your memory later. It can make a valuable keepsake for both of you, but please don't keep it to hold against your

partner at some future date. *It must never be used for negative purposes.*

7. **Keep in mind that the highest purpose here is to lay the foundation for your future marriage, not to tear down what you have already built.** For that reason, some couples find it tremendously helpful to say a short prayer asking for divine guidance before they embark on the journey. There may be times when your partner's thoughts and feelings may catch you totally off guard. You may feel hurt, surprised, or empathetic by some of the things that get revealed. The important thing is to keep the environment safe so that the sharing continues. The last thing you want to do is stop the flow of energy and information. This requires great listening skills and the ability to hold back judgment or criticism. The intention is to stimulate conversation, not criticism. If you criticize or make your partner feel wrong for having their feelings, you will thwart the process. Notice whether or not you are able to simply hear and sit with what your partner has to say. Most of us are great talkers and lousy listeners. When you work on your game plan you will find it helpful to employ what I call the "BLT" technique: Breathe, Listen, and then Talk. It works very well and is helpful in handling many of life's trying situations.

You may also want to give a brief prayer of thanks for your time together at the end of your session. Whether you do or not is completely optional.

8. And finally, however you choose to create it, **reward yourselves at the end of each session.** By the time you

finish sharing so deeply with your partner you might want to take your connection to a physical level. On the other hand, you might want to lighten things up by renting a comedy from the local video store or going to your favorite restaurant. Whatever it is, it should be something on which you both agree. You might agree that he gets to go play pickup basketball with his friends at the park and you get to go ride your Harley with your biker chick friends. Whatever! The point is to reward yourselves, because this can be very intense work.

What follows are just a few topics to get your thoughts stirring. They reflect what I would want to know about in my relationship, but they may be light-years from what's in your game plan. I suggest you read through them for ideas before embarking on your own tailor-made plan.

FAMILY

1. How much involvement are we going to have with our extended families?

2. Are we going to allow certain family members to visit even if one of us has a problem with them? (For example, will your partner's rude and obnoxious uncle, who you can barely tolerate, be welcome to stay the weekend?)

3. Whose family do we spend holidays with, if any? Do we alternate? At whose home will we celebrate?

4. If there are children from previous relationships, what

are our plans for spending time with and caring for them?

5. If there are ex-spouses or ex-partners that are still part of the picture, what role will they play? (This is particularly important if they are the parent of a child from a previous relationship.)

6. Do we like each other's siblings, and, if not, what agreements can we make about their involvement in our lives?

7. Does one of our future in-laws engage in criminal behavior that might taint our relationship? If so, how will we deal with them?

8. Is there a history of abuse in my background? What do I want my partner to know about this and how it has affected me?

9. Is there a history of abuse in your background? What do you want to tell me about it?

10. Is there a history of addiction in either of our backgrounds?

WORK

1. How important is your work to you?

2. Are you willing to support my career aspirations? Even if you don't like them?

3. Do you expect me to work outside of the home?

4. Will we both work outside of the home?

5. If one of us is to be a full-time homemaker, which of us will it be?

6. Does it matter to you what kind of work I do to earn a living?

7. Do I need to consult with you if I want to change careers?

8. Can I quit my job without talking about it with you first?

9. Do you have any expectations of me to attend functions associated with your job?

10. Will our work provide us with enough income to accomplish our financial goals?

11. Are you willing to work at more than one job if necessary?

12. How do you think you might feel if my work thrusts me/us into the public spotlight?

13. If my work requires me to be a public person, do you want to remain outside of the public arena?

14. How much of my time do you expect me to sacrifice in order to help you with your career?

15. Can we both pursue our career goals simultaneously?

16. Will there be a possible conflict between one of our careers and having a family?

MONEY

1. What does money mean to you?

2. Do you believe that there is a correlation between money and happiness?

3. Will we pool our money or keep it separate?

4. How important is saving for the future?

5. Do we need someone to help us with our finances? How will we choose this person and who will communicate with her/him?

6. How much money do you need to feel comfortable? What are our differences in this regard?

7. How much, if any, money will we give to family members?

8. Will we loan money to other people?

9. How hard are we willing to work for money?

10. What are our expectations of each other in contributing

to the family's income? Do you expect me to work? Not to work?

11. Who will handle the monthly bills and financial obligations?

12. How will we provide for any children we might have in the future?

13. Will we each equally contribute to the children's expenses?

14. If one of us is a stay-at-home caretaker, will the other shoulder all the expenses?

15. How will we invest our money? Will we make investment decisions together?

PROPERTY

1. Will all our property be jointly owned?

2. Where will we buy property?

3. Will we purchase artwork or antiques to furnish our home?

4. Will you give me jewelry as gifts or as investment pieces?

5. What type of car(s) will we buy? (luxury or economy)

6. What would it mean to you if we had to declare bankruptcy?

7. How will we decide what is your/my sole property?

8. Is it important to leave property to our children should we have any?

9. How do you feel about the idea of community property?

10. How strongly is your sense of self influenced by what you own?

PETS

1. Is it important to you to have a pet?

2. Did you grow up with pets? What did they mean to you?

3. If we have a pet, who will take care of it?

4. How much are we willing to pay for a pet?

5. How much are we willing to pay to keep the pet alive should something catastrophic happen to it?

6. Are you allergic to any kind of animal?

7. What kind of pets are off limits?

8. Who will care for it when we are on vacation?

9. Should we have only one?

10. Is a pet something that might cause conflict between us? (Example—I like it to sleep on the bed but you don't.)

HEALTH AND FITNESS

1. How important is being fit?

2. Will you find me as attractive if I become overweight?

3. Will you stay with me if I become stricken with a serious illness?

4. How important is our diet?

5. What if one of us is vegetarian or vegan—or if one of our children is?

6. Do you know your family health history?

7. Do you have or have you had any sexually transmitted diseases?

8. Is there any history of illness in your family of origin?

9. Is there anything in your past that might leave either of us susceptible to HIV/AIDS?

10. Have you ever been tested for HIV/AIDS?

11. Have you ever used intraveneous drugs?

12. Have you ever felt suicidal or dealt with serious depression?

13. How will we pay for catastrophic medical expenses?

VACATIONS

1. How much should we spend on vacations?

2. What type of vacations do you prefer? (Climate, destination, activities, etc.)

3. How often would you like to go on vacation?

4. How will we pay for vacations?

5. What has been you favorite vacation experience?

6. What is your dream vacation?

7. How do you feel about taking separate vacations?

8. Do you like to vacation with other couples?

9. What is your worst vacation memory?

10. What makes a vacation good for you?

CHILDREN

1. Do you want to have (more) children?

2. Should we plan when to have children or just leave it up to nature?

3. Whose responsibility is birth control?

4. What was your childhood like?

5. How will we raise our children?

6. How important is it for our children to know their grand-parents and extended family?

7. Can we afford to have children?

8. Are we willing to make the sacrifices necessary to raise children?

9. Are our values aligned when it comes to children?

10. Will we raise our children in a religious way?

11. Should children be spanked?

12. Were you ever abused as a child?

13. What are your memories of your parents as caregivers?

FRIENDS

1. Do I like your friends? Do you like my friends?

2. Are you willing to sever relationships that I think are unhealthy for you?

3. What should we do if either of us is jealous of one of the other's friends?

4. How important are our friends in our life together?

5. Do we have friends that we can depend on under any circumstances?

6. Who is your best friend? Why?

7. Do you consider me a friend as well as a lover?

8. What should I do if I can't stand or don't trust one of your friends?

SEXUALITY

1. How comfortable are you talking about your sexual needs and desires?

2. How important is sex in our relationship?

3. Do you think that our sexual appetites are in sync?

4. How important is monogamy to you?

5. What would it mean to you if I committed adultery?

6. How do you feel about an open relationship?

7. Is sexuality more than sexual intercourse to you?

8. How comfortable do you feel with women's/men's bodies?

9. Is there any relationship between the mind and the body?

10. How comfortable are you with sexual experimentation?

11. What is it about me that you think is sexy?

12. What are your sexual fantasies?

13. What do you consider sexually taboo?

LUXURIES

1. How do you distinguish between a luxury and a necessity?

2. Do you believe that everyone deserves a luxury sometime?

3. What are you willing to do to have something you consider a luxury?

4. Do you expect me to give you expensive gifts? If yes, how often?

5. How will you feel if I cannot afford to give you a life filled with luxury?

RETIREMENT/THE GOLDEN YEARS

1. How do you envision spending our later years?

2. How will we prepare financially for later life?

3. Is it important that we are in good health in our golden years?

4. How active do you hope to be?

5. Will we want to spend time with our children or grandchildren (if applicable)?

6. Do we want to move to a traditional retirement community or live on our own?

7. Do you fear growing old?

8. Will I feel the need to find a younger companion?

9. Is my own value/self-worth based on my youth? Is yours?

10. What will I do to feel useful after I stop working?

VICES

1. Do you do things that might put you or us in jeopardy (an example might be drinking and driving)?

2. Do you like living on the edge or pushing the limits?

3. Do I engage in behavior that might cause you or our family embarrassment?

4. Are some of my associates people with questionable character?

HOUSEHOLD MAINTENANCE

1. Do you believe that the upkeep of a household is the woman's responsibility?

2. What is a fair division of the housekeeping duties?

3. Can we afford to hire help to do the housekeeping?

4. Should we both cook?

5. Will we share expenses for the upkeep of the house?

6. Who will run the errands?

7. Who will shop for groceries?

8. Do you think the woman should work outside the home and also be responsible for the household?

9. How do you feel about a man who stays at home and maintains the household?

10. Is a man any less masculine if he is a househusband?

COMMUNICATION

1. How important is communication to you in our relationship?

2. Will we create our own systems for communicating with each other?

3. Is communication more than talking?

4. Will we seek help when we have difficulty communicating with each other?

5. What was the communication like in your family of origin?

6. How important is communication in a relationship?

7. Do you believe that "actions speak louder than words"?

8. What is the best way to apologize?

9. How difficult is it for me to admit when I have made a mistake?

10. Is it easy for me to share my feelings, or do I withhold them?

Remember, this is just a sample of some of the issues that you and your partner can include in your game plan. If you have specific interests or hobbies, they can be included as well. Your game plan is as individual as you are. One section could have as many as fifty questions. Another might have only two.

Doing this exercise may turn out to be like going to the doctor for your annual checkup. You go in feeling pretty healthy, and indeed by average standards, you are. But after a few in-depth tests you might find out that you need to lose about ten pounds, your blood pressure is slightly elevated, and so too is your cholesterol. They are all things that can be taken care of by a few lifestyle changes, but if left unattended they could have dire consequences. So you have to make a choice: Either get the help you need from your doctor and stick with it, or watch the quality of your health and life decline. That is exactly the same choice you have in your relationship. You may see a few issues that need some attention in order to improve the quality of your relationship. There are many resources you can turn to for help. (You'll find a list of some of the places where you can find help in chapter 5.) Do it for your partner. Do it for yourself. There is no shame in wanting the best relationship possible!

Once your doctor gives you the results of your tests, she will give you a strategy or game plan for losing those unwanted pounds and lowering your blood pressure and cholesterol levels. You know that simply joining a health club and thinking about healthier eating habits is not enough to accomplish your desired result. You have to commit to working out sensibly and regularly in order to lose the weight. You have to actually eat foods that are good for you and forego some of the chips, sodas, and candy bars. You cannot reach your goal by passivity. It requires regular implementation.

So, too, does your game plan for your relationship. Don't let the notebook become a dust collector on your bookshelf. It makes no sense to put in the time and effort to put it together unless you are going to use it regularly. What is regularly? Only you and your partner can determine what feels right for you, but the minimum number of times that I recommend taking it out and going through it thoroughly would be twice a year.

If it makes it easier for you, do it when it's time to change your clocks. Set aside some private, quiet time to review your game plan. Doing it more frequently is preferable because it will keep you in touch with your partner and your goals for your relationship. You may find that the answers to some or many of the questions you formulated initially have now changed drastically. There may be new categories to add to the existing ones. There may be old categories you want to discard or radically modify. A relationship is an ever-evolving entity and so, too, must be your game plan.

Just as with your health game plan, frequency and consistency are essential to meeting your goals. In your health plan you have your doctor and you might also hire a personal trainer or nutritionist to become part of your team. Similarly, if you and your partner find that you are unable to implement the goals you set for yourselves, you might consider seeing a counselor or other individual, such as a clergy member, whom you both trust. Remember, too, that you don't have to make sweeping changes all at once.

Be gentle with yourself and your partner and go as slowly as you need to feel secure and comfortable. You will find your own rhythm and pace.

Having a game plan gives you a road map out of the land of fantasy and naiveté, the land where Powerful Mate Syndrome thrives. It is a tool that will enable you to see that your partner is not a prince, you are not a helpless princess, and there is no such thing as a perfect relationship. It prevents you (and your partner) from glossing over the reality of what will make your relationship thrive or suffer. There is no reason to delude yourself with mistruth, because you have the power within your grasp to make your relationship wonderful and far greater than any fantasy. Now Proceed and Prevail!

7

INVEST IN A PRENUPTIAL AGREEMENT

"Oh, how many torments lie in the small circle of a wedding ring!"
— COLLEY CIBBER, seventeenth-century writer

IN ADDITION to premarital counseling and the formation of a really thorough game plan, I am a big believer in prenuptial (or antenuptial—more on this below) agreements. Why? Aren't they just a weapon rich people use to keep their assets for themselves? The answer is simple. No. If there is any one thing that will shake a woman out of looking at her marriage as a fairy tale and her intended spouse as a prince, it is a prenuptial agreement. More than any other tool, a prenuptial agreement takes the concept of marriage out of the realm of fantasy and into the world of the concrete and tangible. When you are sitting there discussing, crafting, and signing a prenuptial agreement with the person with whom you are pledging to live your life until death do you part, you cannot tell yourself that this is a fairy tale. Suddenly marriage isn't something that will *never* end but rather something that can *definitely* end if the parties in it botch the job. It makes it as real as it can get!

If you're already married but realize after reading this

section that you would like to join those who have chosen to live in reality rather than fantasy, it is not too late. Believe me, an attorney will not turn away the opportunity, and yours can help you draw up an agreement that addresses some issues that you overlooked before you got married. Of course, this is not something that you should do without the knowledge and agreement of your spouse. The last thing that you want to do is create the feeling that you're mounting an offensive against him or her. It can be done civilly and lovingly. Read on to learn why and how to make this important tool work for you.

Cinderella and the prince did not have a prenuptial agreement. They didn't need one, because there was absolutely no possibility they would get a divorce. A prenuptial agreement would have symbolized that each of them had power in the relationship, but that would have been a misrepresentation of the power structure in their relationship. Not only does a prenuptial deal with the division of property in the case of a divorce, it also acknowledges and protects *both* party's interests from the outset—at least that's what a *good* one does. This was the piece of knowledge about prenuptial agreements that I did not have when I needed it most. It should not and need not be a hostile document; it should be a helpful, clarifying tool for *both* parties.

I signed a prenuptial agreement only under duress. Had James and I crafted our agreement together, and had it really represented *both* our interests, perhaps I would not have succumbed to Powerful Mate Syndrome as I did. Certainly, *not* having one that was created in my best interest contributed to my downward spiral.

There are certain days in every person's life that are

unforgettable. August 15, 1984, was one of those days for me. On that day, James presented me with a simple, one-page typed document that stated that his separate property would remain his after our marriage and that the same applied to me. There was also a blank that I was supposed to fill in that stated what dollar amount I would be willing to settle for if the marriage ended in divorce.

I was dumbfounded and nearly speechless—a very rare occurrence in my life! I was so shocked and insulted that I put a big fat zero in the blank and signed it. I had told James numerous times that I was not marrying him for his money and I meant it, but I was so enraged by having this paper thrust at me without discussion that I actually thought about calling off the wedding. However, after I talked with someone whose opinion I valued, I convinced myself that I could learn to live with my pain and that I would eventually "get over it." The wedding went on as planned and, with the exception of James, my confidante, and me, no one knew of the anguish I felt as I recited my vows. In truth, I began my fairy-tale marriage with a broken heart.

James was not entirely to blame for the way this all transpired. True, he was a grown man, but he was also young, naive, and impressionable. He was being coached by a stable of well-meaning attorneys who had represented numerous wealthy clients who had been burned in divorces where there was no prenuptial agreement. However, drafting a good, equitable prenuptial agreement was out of their sphere of expertise. Their interest was in protecting their client, not in coming to an agreement that would serve both of us. They were reactive rather than proactive and didn't have the foresight to see the kind of damage they would inflict on the emotional fiber of our marriage. I guess lawyers don't take an oath like doctors do: "First, do no harm."

Indeed, James and I have differing accounts of how this whole prenuptial situation came about. He says that he asked me if I would sign a prenuptial agreement shortly after we got engaged and that I said, "Sure, it's no problem for me." I honestly don't recall that conversation, perhaps because it was so brief. More likely I dismissed it as a joke! I thought that people had prenuptial agreements only to protect themselves from the person they were marrying, and I didn't think I needed protection from James or he from me.

I think both of us assumed that a prenuptial agreement simply stated what each of us would get if we ever divorced. I know that during the ten months of our engagement, until the day I reluctantly signed off on it, we never discussed a prenuptial agreement again. Neither of us understood what a good prenuptial agreement could be or its potential value to the relationship. Therefore we avoided the issue. That was mistake number one.

The second big mistake that we made was that we did not use the months of our engagement to slowly, methodically work on an agreement. Instead, we talked about the wedding—the guest list, what our attendants would wear, where we would honeymoon, and hundreds of other details. Never was there any in-depth, serious conversation about the marriage, let alone a prenuptial agreement. I simply assumed that it wasn't important to him, and since I did not have any real property to bring into the marriage, I did not see the need for one. I now understand that *every* married couple, regardless of their economic status, should have a prenuptial agreement, but they are especially important when one person has a lot of money and the other has none.

The third mistake we made was not obtaining the assistance and guidance of qualified help in drafting what would eventually become our prenuptial agreement. Neither one of us had any legal background, and this was to be the first marriage for both of us. There was nothing in my background that equipped me to negotiate a contract of any kind with James. He had a stable of lawyers, which is common with professional athletes, to do his bidding. This was the beginning of the adversarial environment. Needless to say, when one party has a team of lawyers and the other party has none, you've got a problem. It was a "them versus me" situation all the way.

If you're cringing right about now, I understand. It's obvious that I didn't want to hear word one about prenups before I married James. I felt as though having an agreement impugned my integrity and that its purpose would be to "keep me in my place." But I was completely ignorant and naive. I believed that the mere existence of a prenup meant that we were dooming the marriage to end before it began. I also felt that having a prenuptial agreement was James's way of saying that he wasn't entirely sure that I was marrying him for love rather than money. And let's face it, it didn't fit into my romantic fantasy at all. I just couldn't figure out why we needed one. I thought that even talking about the legal and financial arrangements would taint the "warm, fuzzy" experience that I was after. However, with time and life experience, I now see that dealing with the hard issues such as money up front is ultimately what *helps* make a marriage warm and fuzzy.

Prenuptial agreements aren't always done in such a loving spirit, it's true, but they can be, and a good agreement can be one of the most constructive tools in your marriage tool kit. Just being willing to sit down together and discuss sensitive issues *before* getting married can be a very loving gesture. It demonstrates the goodwill we have in our hearts for our future life partner. It is about wanting the best for your relationship, being clear about your goals and expectations in the marriage, and being willing to put all your cards on the table.

But first you have to get beyond the desire to see marriage as a fairy tale, and grasp the reality that the issues of money and marriage are inextricably interwoven. Every couple has money issues. Better to be clear from the start than blindsided down the road.

Prenuptial agreements are also much more than simple financial documents. They're about far more than dollars and cents and who gets to keep the prized art collection. At their best, they serve to protect and preserve both parties' rights within the marriage, such as the right to pursue goals and to what extent. If it is going to bankrupt you and your spouse in order to achieve your dream of creating the world's first car fueled by cow manure, should you be able to do that, or should you set some limits on how much you can extract from the family's nest egg? If one of you is passionate about exotic tropical birds but your house is the size of a shoe box, shouldn't there be some limit to how many birds your partner can bring home? A prenuptial agreement can address all those issues. You might laugh now, but sit down one day and watch a couple of episodes of a divorce court show. You will see that these are the kinds of things that couples lock horns about more often than you may have realized. And, yes, prenuptial agreements do cover what will happen should the couple divorce.

So many issues can be worked out in a prenuptial agreement *before* they become problems in a marriage—issues such as how much financial assistance you will give to members of your extended family, and how to provide for your children's future. If one of you attends a twelve-step program, you can write your commitment to continue going to meetings into your prenuptial. Certainly one's commitment to such a program can have a profound effect on a marriage. Perhaps one of you has a long-standing tradition that you celebrate with people other than your spouse.

If this is a second marriage and there are children from a previous relationship, you can put it in your prenuptial agreement that "Peter will spend one month at the summer cabin every year with his daughter Anna until she is eighteen." This could not be changed without "renegotiating." It may seem silly, but it is amazing how manipulative spouses can be when stepchildren are involved. Blended families may benefit in particular from a prenuptial agreement that clearly states everyone's intentions in a document with teeth.

Do either you or your spouse have a valuable collection? Once you're married, does your spouse have the power and authority to sell pieces of the collection or change it in any way? It may seem trivial to you, but what if you get into a financial bind and one of those antique Faberge eggs, if sold on eBay, would bring enough of a windfall to ease your money crunch? What would you do then? A prenuptial agreement that gave that right only to the owner of the collection would prevent a scenario like that from ever occurring.

Of course, if you have already gone through the steps of creating a game plan, you will have covered much of this territory already, but the prenuptial agreement makes things legal, so anything that you would want to have protected by law should be included here as well.

If the tuxedos have all been returned, your bouquet is nicely air dried for posterity, and you are beginning to see some of the more human qualities of your beloved, it's still not too late to create an agreement comparable to a prenup. Essentially, the only thing that is different is its name. If you draft and sign an agreement before you are married, it is called a prenuptial agreement. If it is drafted and signed after you are married, it is called an antenuptial agreement. Even after the wedding's over, you still have tremendous latitude in drafting an agreement where you and your partner are the ultimate authorities.

If you have become accustomed to living without an agreement, it may at first seem strange to begin thinking in the manner that drafting an agreement requires, but if you're committed to the process I outline in the following pages and your intentions are honorable, you will be able to do it. You will also need to decide whether you want to have one attorney work for both of you or each retain your own. The bottom line is that it is never too late to do something beneficial for your relationship as long as the two of you are in agreement that this is what you want to do. If you are already married, just substitute *antenuptial* whenever you see the word *prenuptial* in the pages that follow.

What a Good Prenuptial Agreement Can Do

What the prenup can do is act as a neutral arbiter and relieve you both of having to make such excruciating decisions under pressure. JoAnne and Marcus used their prenuptial agreement in just such a way.

JoAnne and Marcus came to me because they wanted to improve their communication skills. They already had a very good marriage and wanted to do some work to insure that it would stay that way as they moved toward their dream of becoming parents. In my sessions with them, they revealed that they had a prenuptial agreement to which they often referred. They reported that it had served them well. When I asked them in what ways, they pointed out two in particular. First, Marcus has an extensive collection of antique trains. It is a hobby that can be very expensive and also involves travel to conventions all over the country. One of the sections that Marcus and JoAnne put into their prenuptial agreement is a ceiling on how much Marcus can spend on his hobby each year. In addition, they agreed that the trains are Marcus's property exclusively should they ever divorce, regardless of whether or not some of them were purchased with community money.

JoAnne's love is horses. She had one horse, Roosevelt, before she and Marcus married. In the second year of their marriage, they purchased a second horse, Churchill, which technically belongs to both of them. However, because the two horses are inseparable, JoAnne and Marcus added a clause to their already existing agreement which said that the two horses would never be separated and would be considered JoAnne's separate property should they ever divorce.

Their agreement was both a constructive and compassionate tool in their marriage, and it was a living document, changeable as circumstances changed. Through it, they were able to exercise clear judgment about what would be fair and best for everyone involved should they ever divorce.

Having a prenuptial agreement is very similar to carrying health insurance. You don't buy it because you know that someday you are going to be afflicted with a life-threatening, catastrophic illness. Your hope is that you will be healthy and only have to deal with the normal annoyances of getting older. However, should you need it, you have it. It is impossible to get health insurance once you get sick. Likewise, if your marriage breaks down to the point of irreconcilable differences, it is very difficult to be fair and kind to your spouse. And you can forget any kind of civility once the lawyers get involved. If you don't have anything but a potato to split, the lawyers will find a way to turn it into an acrimonious, expensive fiasco.

The way to prevent that from happening is to craft your prenuptial agreement when you are both feeling the most loving toward one another. When goodwill and honorable intentions guide the process, you dramatically decrease the likelihood that you will end up as adversaries. Yes, the process itself can create an adversarial atmosphere, but it doesn't have to.

Drafting a good prenuptial agreement isn't easy, but it doesn't have to be torturous either. Here are a few tips:

First, **take your time.** As soon as you both begin to talk about marriage, begin to incorporate regular discussions about money into your routine. Money is, for most people, a topic more difficult to discuss than sex, and yet it's at the heart of the prenuptial agreement, so give it time. Have bite-sized discussions. You can't expect to cover every issue and feeling you have in one session.

You may discover that you and your partner agree or vehemently disagree about many money issues. Knowing this *before* you get married can only help make your relationship more real and honest. Not knowing simply keeps you on the path of ignorance, and take my word for it, ignorance is not bliss. Ignorance is simply ignorance.

You might find that your partner has very deep-seated ideas about money. Most people do. Ironically, though, most couples would rather talk about any other subject than money and what it signifies to them. It can take time and a lot of patience (and the help of an expert) to work through these complicated issues, but the payoff in terms of the clarity and understanding you gain will be well worth it.

As you discuss what you want to put in your prenuptial agreement, **write down every issue that concerns you both.** Remember, you can include anything in your agreement, no matter how small or inconsequential it might seem.

Only when the two of you believe that you have come to some consensus about what you want in the agreement should you call in the professionals. When I reluctantly signed the piece of paper that was supposed to be our prenuptial agreement, I made the mistake of doing it without the aid of legal counsel. Considering that I got it two days before we got married, I really didn't have time! In hindsight, I understand (all too well, in fact) that I should have made every effort to get a lawyer, even at that late date. But then I would have had to admit to myself that I was not in a fairy tale.

Once you've put all your issues on the table and decided it's time to formalize the agreement, you'll want to look for representation that is:

- *Committed to doing what is in your best interests.* The legal profession oftentimes operates on an adversarial basis. The two of you may have the noblest of intentions when you contact your respective attorneys only to find out after one or two conferences that they have turned your prenup into a personal battle of egos. You have to go to your attorneys with a united front. They work *for* you and the only thing they are needed for is to put your mandates into legal form. It's not their marriage; it's yours.

- *Not interested in creating hostility.* If there is an issue that you and your partner have worked on in your premarital counseling and it has been resolved to the point that you do not feel it needs to be included in your agreement, don't allow either attorney to twist your arm about it. If your lawyer has a problem with her mate not changing the cat's litter box but you don't have that problem with yours, then it's up to you to tell her to leave her issues out of your prenuptial agreement. It is your choice what goes into the prenup, not the attorneys'.

- *Not interested in moving up to the next tax bracket at you and your partner's expense.* Even after you and your partner have made the huge perception shift in how you view your prenuptial agreement and are looking forward to having it crafted and completed, beware of attorneys who will deliberately prolong the process. Why? Because a few more billable hours might mean the difference to him in buying a Mercedes C-class versus a Mercedes E-class. If you already know what you want and need, there is no need to take bread off of your table to put on someone else's.

- *Experienced in crafting prenuptial agreements.* Just like finding the right therapist, so too will finding the right attorney to craft your prenuptial agreement probably require a bit of research. The time you invest, though, will pay dividends later. Your counselor may be able to give you a recommendation. Your local chapter of the American Bar Association may be a terrific source for referrals. Again, the yellow pages are a good place to begin your search. Find several family law attorneys willing to grant you a consultation so that you can begin to weed out candidates. A local law school, particularly one with a faculty member with experience in prenuptials, is probably a good option. These days there are even low-cost legal services where a paralegal can assist you in preparing your own documents.

Lastly, never lose sight of the fact that you and your partner are a team. Even members of the same team have to scrimmage against one another at times in order to keep the team strong. The period of time that you devote to your prenuptial agreement should be viewed as simply a scrimmage that will prepare you to take on the challenges of marriage as a united, formidable team. Keep that uppermost in your mind, and both of you will be greatly rewarded.

One of the things I never realized before I got married

was how intricately interwoven my need for a career of my own was with my happiness in my marriage. It never occurred to me how much a prenuptial agreement could have helped me both preserve my personhood and openly declare that working was a condition of marriage for me. I cannot explain why I, the woman who grew up wanting to be like Barbara Walters and Barbara Jordan, suddenly, with the utterance of a few marriage vows, transformed myself into little more than an indentured servant. As my former husband would so succinctly tell me in later years on the occasions when I practically begged for some acknowledgement of how I had cooked and cleaned so many years, "I never asked you to do that." And the real truth is that he didn't. My years of princess indoctrination did. I wrongly assumed that that was what a "good wife, a.k.a. princess" was supposed to do!

For a person like myself who believes in putting goals on paper and keeping journals, writing a declaration of how both James and I would support my career aspirations would have been a great help in empowering me. Some of the statements could have read like this:

1. Angela will retain the services of a life/career coach to help her create a game plan for achieving her career goals.

2. Angela will enroll in some form of education-graduate school in broadcasting, acting classes, etc. that will help further her career goals.

3. The duties of running the household will be delegated

to a person agreed upon and hired by both Angela and James.

4. James will be responsible for getting his meals on game days. (He had always done this before, but once we got married I assumed it was my duty.)

5. Angela will only attend James's ball games if they fall on a weekend. (I thought I was supposed to be at every game regardless of what I had going on in my life.)

6. James will be responsible for his own transportation to and from the airport for road trips. (He had always done this for himself before we were married. Again, I assumed that I was now the transportation captain.)

Some of you are probably thinking that those things simply should have been said when we got married, but they were not. Assuming is commonplace with couples, which is what gets us in trouble later on when we start wondering why our mate didn't instinctively know or do something that we wish they had. Having those things in our prenuptial agreement would have made it so that we were both aware of how much it meant to me to achieve my goals. It also would have made clear that it was up to both of us to support them: Me by getting out in the world and going for it, and James by understanding that I wouldn't be the traditional sports wife who is there to wait on her man at all times.

The world of sports is somewhat of an anomaly, but the same ideas about declaring the importance of a woman's career can be said for any woman married to a powerful man in a career where the wife is counted as one of his "assets." Think of Hillary Clinton, torn between being First Lady and pursuing her own goals independent of that role. Any woman married to a person in a large corporate structure knows how important "the wife" is in office politics. If you just assume that your spouse has your interests and goals uppermost in his mind, you may be in store for a rude awakening. Maybe you have a career or hobby that requires you to be away from home frequently. You assume that it will be a nonissue with your spouse, but after a few months of you being gone so much he declares that you've got to find something to do that keeps you closer to home. You are devastated. Doesn't he understand the importance of this to you? The time and place to make it known is in the prenuptial agreement!

I don't want to oversimplify the issue, but I suggest that you think of your marriage as a huge feast: one that will last year after year. It (the prenuptial agreement) is the master "recipe," composed of many smaller recipes (all your issues that have been fleshed out), which will enable you to carry off the feat of a successful feast. Time spent considering every detail, every contingency, every conceivable crisis creates a greater likelihood of success than failure. Both you and your partner can emerge feeling loved, honored, and satisfied. That is exactly the way I want those who sit around my Thanksgiving table to feel at the end of our time together.

In reality, there *can* be such a thing as a great prenuptial agreement—one that serves you and your partner equally well. It can be yours if that is what you are committed to. When it is finished you can store it in a safe place along with your will (another important document that both you and your partner must have). They are both documents that you will need to revisit as the circumstances of your life change, and, if all goes well, one of you will be reading the will before the prenuptial agreement.

Finally, although I have been stressing the point that there is no one-size-fits-all, I'd like to leave you with a list of issues that I have found to be critical to all prenuptial agreements. These eighteen issues represent only a starting point of what is possible for inclusion in your prenuptial agreement, but I urge you to consider each one very carefully before you sign on the dotted line.

THE EIGHTEEN ISSUES EVERY PRENUPTIAL AGREEMENT SHOULD ADDRESS

1. How will you determine which funds are separate and which are joint? Will you each keep what you earn after you are married as your separate property, or will you pool some of it?

2. Are you both going to contribute to the household budget and upkeep?

3. If only one of you generates income from sources outside of the home, will the party who does not have an equal say in how it is used?

4. If one of you receives an inheritance, will you share it equally or is it the recipient's separate property?

5. How will real estate purchases be held: as joint or separate property?

6. If one of you has a pet before you get married, whose responsibility is it to care for it after you're married? What if you both become very attached to it and you end up divorcing? Who gets the pet then? What if you buy two pets during the marriage and subsequently divorce? What happens to the pets?

7. Are you going to live on a budget?

8. Is there a limit to what one party may spend without having to consult the other party? (Keep in mind that some hobbies and habits can be prohibitively expensive!)

9. Does either party permit casual drug or alcohol use? If one of you feels very strongly about this, it can become a major source of discord in your relationship.

10. What about having children? Should you both agree to take responsibility for birth control? What if one of you is completely opposed to having children?

11. Whose responsibility is it to support children from previous relationships who might live with you?

12. Will you agree to continue to go to counseling at regularly scheduled intervals for relationship tune-ups? (It could be once a month or once every three months. It could also be in the form of a relationship retreat you do together once a year.)

13. How much intervention in your relationship will you

tolerate from other family members? Where are the boundaries between parents-in-law, siblings, and other extended family members?

14. How will you decide to say no to people who ask you for money? Will you hire someone specifically to do that unpleasant job or will one of you handle it?

15. What are the absolute nonnegotiable issues in the marriage for you? For your partner?

16. Will you hire professional help to manage your affairs? If so, how will you choose them? Which of you has the power to change or fire such persons?

17. Will you agree to stop any life-threatening activities with which your mate is uncomfortable? If not, how will you resolve the issue?

18. Do you expect your mate to stay married to you if you should become incapacitated mentally or physically?

A little piece of the idealist still lives within me. I hope that death will be the only thing that causes you to part ways. However, if your marriage ends in divorce, a good prenuptial agreement will prevent you from having to go through protracted and expensive shenanigans like I did. Ironically, the prenuptial agreement that I was so afraid of would have saved me years of my time, hundreds of thousands of dollars, and many sleepless nights. It turned out that the thing that I feared would hurt me most could actually have helped me most.

I cannot overstate the importance not only of the agreement itself but of all the discussion and work that goes into it. Doing all this exploring *before* you get married will help you get in touch with your position as an empowered and equal partner in your relationship and it will help solidify your relationship as one based in reality rather than fantasy. That's a preventive for Powerful Mate Syndrome if I ever heard one. Proceed and Prevail!

As your "reality" godmother, here is my advice for you: The best way to mitigate the damage and destruction in the event of a disaster is adequate preparation. If you live in an area that is prone to earthquakes, you purchase earthquake insurance and you keep a supply of flashlights, batteries, canned food, water, and other necessities on hand. You also educate yourself about the proper procedures to follow when one hits.

The same proactive behavior is necessary as it relates to your marriage. A good prenuptial agreement is earthquake insurance for your marriage. You may never need it, but it's better to have it and not need it than to need it and not have it.

8

MAKE AND MANAGE
YOUR OWN MONEY

"A fool and [her] money are soon parted." —adage

WE TOUCHED briefly on money in the previous two chapters, but this book would be incomplete without a fuller exploration of this touchiest of subjects. Let's face it, money and all that it symbolizes is often much harder to talk about than almost any other issue, including sex. Perhaps that's why it was in the area of money that I felt the insidious effects of Powerful Mate Syndrome most acutely. We just didn't talk about it. Clearly it takes more than having access to money to have real power, but the price of not dealing with the issue of money is far higher than a little discomfort.

Every day I hear stories about women who go on ridiculous shopping sprees, spending money as if they have their own personal mint, looking for some sense of power in a thousand-dollar designer handbag or in hundreds of pairs of shoes. Sometimes the search for power leads to the jewelry store because we've somehow come to equate the number of carats you can afford with the amount of power you have. I've been one of those women, and I've worked with a number of clients who are, too. Believe me, there are a lot of women walking around dripping with diamonds who don't feel powerful. I had a jewelry box filled with them, my closet was bulging with beautiful designer clothing, and the luxury sedan was parked in the garage. I went through a lot of shoes, cars, jewelry, and other material things to finally figure out that people who really have power are not the ones flaunting their buying power. The people with real power understand their financial situation and take a proactive role in managing it.

Regardless of whether a couple is living paycheck to paycheck or they are millionaires, they often struggle with some of the same issues. They may be dealing in different dollar amounts, but they're both dealing with the effects of a lack of communication and a lack of knowledge. That is a fact that needs to change for the well-being of both women and men.

I learned the hard way the importance of managing one's finances intelligently and how doing so leads to a feeling of empowerment. I also learned the repercussions of not managing one's finances. In hindsight, I see how my lack of action and my mistaken belief that I was powerless resulted in my being less secure financially than I should have been.

When I married James I became the prototypical "Seabiscuit" wife. I put on blinders and blocked out any and everything that did not fit my idea of my fairy-tale marriage. Part of that fairy tale was believing that my prince would not only earn the money to support the household but also have the knowledge and wherewithal to take care of it. It is amazing how I managed to convince myself of these things when underneath I always believed that I should be taking care of myself. Now that I have a background in psychology, I liken what happened to me to what happens to people who grow up as victims of child abuse. They tell themselves, "I will never hit my children when I become a parent," but ironically it is often adults who were abused as children who become the perpetrators of more abuse. I lived with feelings of ambivalence and anxiety about this for most of my married life. I thought that I was doing the right thing by acting like a princess, and yet I was mired in self-loathing for doing so.

One of the most galling things about Powerful Mate Syndrome is that even the most intelligent, self-assured woman can come to believe that she should give up control of nearly everything because she has a mate who can and will do it all. For many of us, especially today, this runs counter to the expectation we had that we would earn our own money and were capable of taking care of ourselves. My role models were all women who worked, and part of my dream was to follow their lead, but somewhere in my young adulthood that dream got displaced. In its place I put the image of James that I saw out in the world—the powerful, capable of doing everything, calm-under-pressure man who would be just as adept (or even more adept) at handling our financial situation as he was in every other aspect of his life.

The prince will take care of everything, right? Wrong! First of all, we were not living in a fairy tale. True, James was playing professional basketball—a world that can seem like a fairy tale at times. Nevertheless, it is a career that is usually very short lived, even if you are a star and you can avoid any serious injuries. Second, neither James nor I came to the marriage with any experience in handling the kind of money he was making. A couple of hundred dollars is one thing, a couple of million is a horse of a different color. Third, my belief that as long as we had lots of money we wouldn't need to talk about it was as far from reality as one can get. The fact is, having money is all the more reason to talk about it, especially if you want to keep some of it. Because we had both come from backgrounds where a little more money in the coffers would have made life easier for our families, we both came to the unfounded conclusion that as long as we had lots of money, we were assured of having a happy life. We are living proof of the adage, "A fool and his money are soon parted."

I feel compelled to say that I am not blaming James for my lack of action during that time or the financial situation that I find myself in now. I am far from living on skid row, but I certainly could have done a lot better at managing our money. I see too many women who, like myself, sabotage themselves financially by relying on their princes to be the breadwinners in the family, to single-handedly manage the finances, and to provide for all their needs in later life. That is what we do, whether intentional or not, when we buy into the idea of the fairy tale and the omniscient prince. Every circumstance in my life today is the result of choices I made or did not make while I was afflicted with Powerful Mate Syndrome. I take full responsibility for the way my life has played out. That is precisely why I have made it my mission to wake up other women who are putting their hopes in a nonexistent fantasy.

Powerful Mate Syndrome tells us that we can turn over the concern about and control of money to our powerful partner. He will capably determine the direction of our financial future. That is simply another way that we become coconspirators in diminishing our power. Let's face it. Women can no longer give up their interest in the financial issues of their families. The days when men handled all the finances and made all the decisions fell by the wayside forty years ago. The only thing that is accomplished by a woman giving up her interest in the financial affairs of her family and leaving it all up to her husband is the perpetuation of the myth of the "Powerful Prince" and the fairy tale. Not only that, she is also unfairly burdening her partner, who may be less capable than she of handling the responsibilities of finance management.

Women have proven that they are just as capable as men of handling the family money. I was in denial about that back in the days when I was married. I listened to our accountant (and I use that term loosely) who convinced me that one sign of "having made it" was not having to be concerned with our financial matters. I don't believe for one minute that Oprah Winfrey subscribes to the belief that "making it" means you can afford to turn a blind eye to your financial affairs. The true sign of having made it would have been me keeping close track of our income, investing it wisely, and screening the people we entrusted with the money more closely.

Whether you stay married for fifty years or you get divorced after one or two, you must give up the fantasy that your partner will always take care of the money and finances. The longer you tell yourself that your prince has everything under control, the longer you keep yourself in the dark, and the more you limit your ability to exercise power over your own life. Knowing how to manage your money and being informed about your financial health is an essential part of ridding yourself of Powerful Mate Syndrome, and of becoming a strong and fully realized individual.

Take an Active Role

I think it is a huge mistake for any woman in modern times to expect her mate to handle all the financial matters for the family without her help and input. You not only have the right but also the *responsibility* to know everything about your finances. Anyone who tells you that the path to a happier, more intimate relationship with your mate begins when you give up your interest and control in the money matters is not in touch with the reality of relationships. They are stuck in their own version of a fairy tale which says that you have to be less of who you are in order to get more from your relationship. I say hogwash! That may have been true a hundred years ago, but in the words of Ann Richards, the former governor of Texas, in the twenty-first century "that dog won't hunt."

It's the equivalent of saying that married women shouldn't learn how to drive if they have a husband who drives, because he can take them anywhere they need to go. Both ideas do nothing but put the woman in a subordinate position to her mate. If God had intended for woman to be subordinate to man, he would have made her out of a toe, not a rib! There is nothing beautiful, inspiring, or empowering about being subordinate to or dependent on your mate. The goal is to be interdependent, meaning that the success of your relationship depends on each of you to contribute your time, attention, and talents to it.

In my marriage, all I really had to do was learn enough to manage the people who were managing our money. But I didn't know that. I did not have to have an M.B.A or know how to trade stocks and purchase mutual funds or negotiate huge blockbuster real estate deals. Some basic knowledge, a discerning eye, and some intelligent, probing questions each month would have sufficed—at least in the beginning. At the very least I needed to realize that the money James earned was just as much mine as it was his and that I had just as much right and responsibility to take on its steward-ship. For heaven's sake, *one* of us needed to step up and be the caretaker of our family finances. James and I lived as though we had an entire orchard of money trees growing in our backyard. It wasn't until I began divorce proceedings that it became clear just how mangled our finances were. No, I let my fear of dealing with numbers and the belief that "it really wasn't *my* money" stop me. And I regretfully admit that that didn't stop me from spending it foolishly either.

Whenever I think about that period in my life, I am re-minded of a line from one of my favorite movies. In *People Will Talk*, Cary Grant's character, Dr. Noah Praetarious, says, "The things people do when they're afraid to be afraid," re-ferring to the lengths to which we will go in order to avoid facing the fear we feel in so many areas of life. You may know all too well that your relationship is dysfunctional, but that doesn't mean you aren't terrified at the thought of leaving it. You are afraid to be afraid. Instead, you sacrifice your health and happiness. Being afraid to be afraid used to be a way of life for me. I have since learned that it's okay to be afraid. It is not okay to let that stop you from doing what you know in your gut is the right thing to do. (It's ironic, though, that this particular movie is also something of a Cinderella story, so deeply rooted in our society's collective unconscious are the archetypes of the "prince" and the "damsel in distress.")

If it seems that I am putting too great an emphasis on money in a relationship it is because money is pivotal in *every* relationship. It symbolizes, among other things, power. Except in the rarest of cases, the person in charge of the money—or the one who is at least aware of where it is and its status—is the person with the power in the relationship. Nothing is a better power equalizer than having *both* spouses share the responsibility and the knowledge about the family's finances. It's also a good predictor of whether power is shared well in other areas of the relationship.

<u>Your Separate, Not Secret, Stash</u>

During my marriage, I had the privilege of getting to know one of the Lakers wives, a woman named Charlina McAdoo. Charlina was married to Bob McAdoo, who, like James and myself, attended the University of North Carolina at Chapel Hill. Also like us, they had strong family ties in North Carolina.

Charlina was a beautiful woman, but she was not about to be any man's trophy wife. None of that "wives should be seen and not heard" rhetoric for her! She was intelligent, ambitious, effervescent, kind, and funny, but what I remember most was that she possessed wisdom about life that was beyond her years. She was a woman who told it like it was in every situation. Charlina succumbed to cancer at an early age, but I will never forget one of the things she told me. She said, "No matter how wonderful your marriage is, you always need to have some money set aside in your name and your name only. You should be able to put your hands on it at a moment's notice. It doesn't need to be a secret stash, just separate from the money that you and your man have together." I listened to her, but I didn't think her advice applied to me. Why? Because I was married to the prince, and I was living the ultimate fairy tale. "There is no way that James and I will ever break up and that I will need any separate money," I thought as she spoke. It wasn't until many years after her death, as my marriage was on the rocks, that I realized how right she had been. By then, however, I had a full-blown case of PMS and had given up practically all my power over my financial destiny.

I once had a client who made the dangers of financial dependence all too clear. She sought me out specifically because of my past experience as the wife of a professional athlete. Her husband played professional football. One day she recounted to me a game when he had put in a particularly exasperating performance. From experience she suspected that she might be in for a "difficult" night. To make a long, ugly story short, he ended up pummeling her to make up for his lousy performance earlier that day. After he used her as a punching bag, he wanted to have "make-up" sex. She complied. She admitted that she tolerated his temper and abuse because the lifestyle that he afforded her was something that she had always dreamed of growing up in her barely middle-class neighborhood; she did not want to give up the special treatment that went along with being his wife. It took a broken jawbone to convince her that it was time to cut her losses before they included her life.

The physical abuse in this story might make it an extreme example, as might the couple's large bank account. Regardless of the specifics of your emotional, physical, and financial situation, you should not rely on your partner for sole financial support.

In some ways, having your own financial power and separate stash enables you to determine your own fate. If you are fortunate and never need to tap this reservoir, you can either leave it to someone in your will or go out in your golden years and buy yourself a fabulous motorcycle, take lessons on how to ride it, and then strike out on a cross-country road trip through the United States. The point is, if you do need it, (especially in the case of escaping physical violence) and you don't have it, unfortunate or even tragic outcomes could result.

There I go again taking the romance out of the fairy tale, but we all need to acknowledge that such possibilities exist—for all of us. I want to say unequivocally that James never hit me during our relationship, but we all know that there are a lot of princes who don't think twice about inflicting physical abuse upon their princesses. There are circumstances under which it becomes unbearable to continue chasing the fairy tale, and women have to leave their homes. There is no sweet or subtle way to say it. It is one of the painful realities of our world.

The Price of Inattention

There is one thing that fairy tales and reality tales have in common, and that is that wolves exist in both. By wolves I mean the people who are always around encouraging you not to pay attention to, or become involved with, your financial matters. There are lots of wolves out there lurking about in human form—and I don't mean your partner. Sometimes it behooves the princess to become the protector, not the protected one. I meet women all the time who tell me that they thought their husband was managing their money only to find out later that they'd been cleaned out by their trusted money manager. Not just well-to-do people, either. Middle-class couples who don't pay attention to what their financial planner is doing or to the bit of money they have invested in the stock market are in the same boat.

The bottom line is that no matter how much or how little money you have, keep your hands on the reins and make it your business to know what is going on. No one other than you and your partner ought to have carte blanche over your money and financial matters. Anyone else needs to get your permission or approval to make decisions involving your money. Nobody is ever going to take better care of you than you can yourself. Get over the need to have someone else be responsible for your life.

Get a Job!

Perhaps I have put the cart before the horse. In order to manage money, of course you've got to have some in the first place! By now I'm sure it's clear that I believe every woman should work and have her own source of income. Just as important as the income that working produces is the sense of accomplishment and satisfaction that work can provide. It doesn't matter if your partner is barely making ends meet or needs a Brink's truck to carry his money to the bank; unless you are doing something in your life that makes you feel good, what he's worth is worthless to you. His money might buy you Botox, Manolo Blahniks, and a Bentley, but it cannot buy you a soul! Eleanor Roosevelt said, "When you cease to make a contribution, you begin to die."

I am talking about work that not only supports you if you need it, but also makes a contribution to others and this planet. It doesn't have to be a high-paying job. In fact, if you are financially secure, you could volunteer doing something you love. But do consider the money side. You might not need the paycheck now, but you would be surprised how many women who thought they were set for life financially go through a life-altering experience and end up living just above poverty later on. When you earn enough to support yourself, you free yourself to make choices in your own best interest and those of your children.

Establishing Credit

There is one last topic I want to cover before we leave this discussion about money and finances, and that is credit and creating a credit history. The woman who doesn't need credit is a woman who doesn't need oxygen. Every woman needs her own credit and, hence, her own credit history. In some states, creditors and lenders are mandated to record transactions in both parties' names if you are married, but I wouldn't count on that. I firmly believe that you need to establish *your own credit history separate and apart from your spouse.* You may never need it, but it is better to have it and not need it than to need it and not have it. I can already hear some of you saying, "But why should I bother with establishing a credit history when my husband provides for all my needs?"

The short answer is that the world now deals in credit, not cold hard cash. And although it sounds clichéd, getting credit can be the classic catch-22—if you don't have it you can't get it and you can't get it unless you already have it. Unless you establish your own credit you may end up like my pug who's always trying to catch her curly tail but it's always just out of reach.

Now, don't accept every credit card offer you get in the mail. You don't need (or want) a stack of credit cards in your pocket, and running up huge piles of credit debt is foolish. What you need to do is establish a *good* credit history. If your partner is always the one who makes credit purchases, then he'll be the one with the credit history. You need to have at least one credit card in your name only, or jointly make a purchase that will list you and only you as the responsible party. You don't need a ten-thousand-dollar credit limit on a card that charges eighteen percent interest. If you should choose to go the route of making a purchase, it doesn't have to be a house or a Lamborghini. Something simple and inexpensive will do just as nicely as long as you finance it and make the payments in a timely fashion. Choose a card with no annual fee and a low interest rate. Use it every now and then to get your history started, but use it wisely.

Having your own credit history does not mean that you have some clandestine plan to leave your mate someday or that you are preparing for the worst to happen in your relationship. It is a lot like having car insurance. Just because you have it doesn't mean that you're destined to be in an accident. However, if you do have an accident you can rest assured knowing that your assets are covered. If, heaven forbid, your mate were to drop dead and he was the only one with a credit history, you might find yourself in a difficult situation. This is true even if you have lots of cash on hand. Credit is a fact of life. Cinderella may not have needed a credit history, but you definitely do! Today it is an integral part of keeping your financial power intact.

You can't risk having to get your spouse's blessing, permission, or whatever to green light your ability to purchase something. Knowing that you have the ability to get what you need for yourself is a tremendous part of avoiding the scourge of Powerful Mate Syndrome. In the next chapter you will take your program for empowerment to the next level.

9

GOD, GRACE, AND GRATITUDE

"What you appreciate appreciates."

—DR. REV. MICHAEL BECKWITH

VANESSA WILLIAMS, the talented actress, singer, mother, and also the wife of a successful and powerful partner, sings one of my favorite songs, "Save the Best for Last," which describes how I feel about this chapter. It focuses on what I believe are three of the most important "tools" that you will need to help make your relationship impervious to the effects of Powerful Mate Syndrome: God, grace, and gratitude. Rather than your relationship being a morass of confusion, lost identity, and lack of purpose, they can help you make your time in the role of the significant other to a powerful partner most satisfying and beneficial for you.

One of the things that made me vulnerable to Powerful Mate Syndrome was that I had a major disconnect from God. Although I was raised in the Methodist church and spent my whole life in one kind of church or another, these days I prefer to refer to myself as a "spiritual Heinz 57." That is a fancy way of saying that I am a spiritual mutt. I take solace and inspiration from a wide variety of spiritual coaches, religions, and writings. It is not my goal to sway

92

you in the direction of any particular religion; only to have you acknowledge that there is a "Source" greater than you or me. You can call it anything you like. As long as you are connected to something greater, you will always have an ally in the battle against Powerful Mate Syndrome.

Somewhere between the summer of 1984 and the winter of 1994, I lost sight of my "Source." I, like so many women who succumb to PMS, began to make two critical errors in my thinking. First, I began to worship my powerful partner as the source of all that was good in my life. He gave me love, he provided a home for me, he supplied me with over-flowing material riches, and his career was a source of endless excitement. He became my god. It wasn't as if I made altars to him or burned incense to honor him, but I *did* stop thanking and acknowledging the *real* source of both his and my blessings, a source I choose to call "God."

I took the abundance of material goods in my life as proof of God's love and blessings. I was living in a custom-built, ten-thousand-square-foot house situated on beautiful, park-like grounds, complete with a gigantic swimming pool and spa. In the three-car garage were his and hers Mercedes Benzes and a nicely equipped minivan that our live-in nanny used to transport the children. I had accumulated material riches beyond what I had ever imagined, and I took this to mean that I had everything I needed in my life. I never longed for the company of others, because in addition to all the "stuff" I possessed, I had all the friends and acquaintances that *money* could buy. We could get reservations in any hot spot in L.A. and we got VIP treatment wherever we went. This was further proof to me that God is good. Well, wisdom is sometimes hard-earned. It would take years and a major fall from my high horse to make me realize that I was using the wrong litmus test for determining God's goodness and presence in my life.

I made James, the conduit for all this goodness, a kind of substitute for God. We are all susceptible to taking what we see our powerful mates do out in the world and attributing to them powers that are beyond those of mere mortals. I'm not talking solely about famous athletes, entertainers, or other public figures. Think of the number of ministers in small communities who become like God to their congregation, especially to the women. It happens very easily because we are always looking for a hero, a savior of some kind, a prince. When we turn men into princes, we set them up to fail. I had completely unreasonable expectations of my powerful mate. Many of us do. Hold on. Before you start screaming that I'm letting men off the hook: I'm not giving anyone a pass to do anything they want with impunity. Integrity, honesty, and self-control are all things that you should expect from your partner in a committed relationship. *Those* qualities are humanly possible. God-like power is not.

It took a series of events and losses to jolt me back to the reality that there was something or someone greater than James or me that was the source of all that I had, all that I was, and all that I could be. I can't tell you the exact moment, but ultimately I realized that "the Source" was still surrounding me, even when the house had been sold, the cars were gone, the "friends and acquaintances" had disappeared, and my marriage was irreparably damaged. Even in the darkest of days, when I watched my life as I had come to know it slowly crumble before my eyes, there was still a glimmer of hope, an irrepressible flame.

That flame was God. Now don't misunderstand me. I'm not saying go out and forsake all your worldly goods and end your relationship with your powerful mate. I'm just telling you that *he is not God.* He is a gift to you from God or the Source or whatever you want to call "It," but don't strap your hopes for a great life on the back of your powerful partner as if he is some kind of pack mule. *It is not his responsibility to carry your burdens or to fulfill your dreams.* That is another remnant of the fairy tale that leads to Powerful Mate Syndrome. Rather, find your "Source" and deposit your dreams there. Then, with your Source as your ally, go ahead and build your human relationship with your mortal mate, sidestepping the traps of PMS.

Grace

One of the things that I did not realize before I married James was just how much the public would recognize me or know about my life. No, there were not articles in the newspaper about me, yet often when I was out and about town, people would recognize me and want to stop and chat about James, our dogs, or the team. I always enjoyed meeting people and I kept in mind what my mom used to say, "Always treat everyone with respect, because the same people that you meet on your way up might be the same ones you meet on your way down." I never lost sight of the fact that it was the fans, particularly the ones who bought seats so high up in the arena that they practically needed oxygen tanks and who showed up whether the team won or lost night in and night out, to whom I owed a great deal of gratitude. They deserved my respect.

Yes, I was in a situation that very few people will ever experience, but the lesson is the same for any woman who is in a relationship with a powerful partner. You are a role model whether you choose to be or not, and as such you must always comport yourself with grace. What does grace have to do with Powerful Mate Syndrome? This is the correlation: When you are in a relationship with a powerful mate, it is very easy to feel insignificant and powerless. Your partner is always the center of attention. You begin to think that no one sees you, no one knows you are alive, and no one cares. But you are mistaken. When your mate is a powerful person, people are watching you whether you know it or not. Powerful Mate Syndrome will make you think otherwise, but believe me, they are. People are always interested in the spouse or significant other of a powerful person. If you have grace and graciousness in your "life tool kit," they will help you to get outside of your vision of yourself as insignificant, powerless, and as a shadow or appendage of your mate. Perhaps Francis Bacon said it best: "If a man be gracious and courteous to strangers, it shows he is a citizen of the world, and that his heart is no island cut off from other lands, but a continent that joins them." (Just substitute woman for man!)

My point is simply that I believe you will find, when you show grace to others, you empower yourself. I don't think this has ever failed to be true. Come on—this doesn't have to turn into quantum physics. You don't need me to draw you a map of what most of us have been told since we were toddlers, "Do unto others as you would have them do unto you."

What does that have to do with Powerful Mate Syndrome? I'll tell you what. I don't have empirical data to back up my next statement. It comes strictly from my gut and my experiences with other women who have had Powerful Mate Syndrome. If you are not careful, PMS will turn you into the biggest witch that you have ever known, and the kicker is that you won't even realize it. (Some people would find the word that rhymes with *witch* more appropriate, but I think that word is too often used to keep powerful women under control, subordinate, and questioning their right to exercise their power, so I prefer *witch*.) A witch is nasty, mean-spirited, and coldhearted. That's what happens to a woman hardened by Powerful Mate Syndrome. But grace, more specifically, showing grace to others, helps to keep your heart and spirit out of the deep freeze. I believe that it's all connected: feeling powerless and being unable to show grace to others go hand in hand.

When I used to go to auditions I was keenly aware that the actors who felt small, threatened by the competition, inadequate, and just plain scared were always the ones who blew into the waiting room with great fanfare, running their mouths a thousand miles an hour, talking loudly on their cell phones, and doing all those things that said, "Look at me: I'm somebody." What they were doing in actuality, rather than making a statement, was asking a question—"I am somebody, aren't I?" By contrast, the more accomplished actors, some with very recognizable faces and long, impressive lists of credits, were friendly, generous, and much more subdued. They embodied grace. You can too. So just *be nice!* I didn't say be a doormat. I said be nice.

Gratitude

My treatise on gratitude is short, but that should not be taken as an indication that I think it is of lesser importance than the others. During the time that I struggled with Powerful Mate Syndrome, I also failed to express gratitude for all that was present in my life. Not only had I exiled God from my life, I didn't express any gratitude to anyone—human or divine—for all that I had, be it a letter in the mail from an old friend, a romp in the backyard with the dogs, or an opportunity to visit the White House. I became completely oblivious to the fact that all these wonderful things didn't just happen in a vacuum.

Being grateful is not a matter of religion. You can be an agnostic and still feel gratitude. I keep a passage from one of my favorite books, *Altars* by Denise Linn, on the desk where I write to remind me of the importance of gratitude. It says, "Appreciation for the bounty and blessings in life is one of the most effective ways of increasing these qualities. Being grateful for the goodness in your life creates a kind of magnetic attraction for even more blessings to come your way. Gratitude helps you be receptive to the life force of the universe."

Expressing gratitude is appropriate not only for the good times but also for the hard times. Why? Because when you are expressing gratitude for anything, you don't have the time or the void in your life to feel powerless. The two cannot exist in the same time and space. Try it. You'll see for yourself.

When I was at the lowest point of my life, completely engulfed by Powerful Mate Syndrome, I was not grateful for anything. I could not begin to see the value in dealing with the disintegration of my family life, or with my feelings of betrayal, depression, and a whole host of other unpleasant experiences. I didn't realize that, "Steel comes from a fiery furnace," as Edward G. Robinson says in the movie *Unholy Partners*. I am so grateful for all the wonderful adventures that I had as a result of being married to James, but I am equally grateful for "the fire," because I am wiser, more compassionate, smarter, definitely stronger, and truly grateful for all that I have and have become. Now I am that "steel" of whom Robinson spoke, but I am steel with a grateful heart.

I believe that there is a spiritual component to overcoming PMS. As long as you wallow in negativity and inaction, the more of it you will manifest. On the other hand, when you begin to express gratitude for everything in your life—the good, the bad, and the ugly—you will begin to clear the space in your psyche to begin the reclamation of your life. You are in for a fascinating journey back to yourself. Proceed and Prevail!

PART THREE

RECLAIMING

YOUR POWER

If you have read this far, you've probably decided at least three basic things:

• that you no longer want to live your life chasing an elusive fairy tale
• that life as a "princess" isn't all it's cracked up to be
• that you are ready to do the work required to reclaim your life

Take it from me, there is no magic wand on this end of the tale either. There isn't a fairy godmother who can magically erase all the trauma and drama that you have experienced on your way here. No, there's just me, the "reality godmother," who believes in telling you the things you *need* to hear, not necessarily the things you *want* to. I do have some good news, too, and that is that *you have the power within yourself, no matter how exhausted or frustrated or disillusioned you might feel, to reclaim your strength and purpose.*

Many of you fear that reclaiming your life means having to say good-bye to your relationship. Nothing could be further from the truth. The only goal of this process is to help you become a better you. A better you makes everything and everyone you are a part of better. My hunch is that if you went to your partner and said the following, something interesting would happen: "Honey, I realize that I have made you responsible for making me happy and giving me a challenging and fulfilling life for all these years. I am now relieving you of this duty that I unfairly thrust upon you. I am now taking responsibility for my own happiness. Your responsibility now is to be the best person you can possibly be and the best partner I could ever have." If you said this, he might stop dead in his tracks and wonder what in the world had happened to the "old" you. And he'd be delighted. You see, I don't believe that most men want to be burdened with being the alpha and omega to their wives. It is something that gets put upon them by our culture, which craves princes larger than life who can slay evil forces, save a life with a kiss, and still be tender and loving. I know that the men in our lives, our "princes," are just as hurt as we are by perpetuating these ideas of "the prince" and "the princess" and "happily ever after." Let's move beyond fantasy and into reality.

You don't need to be a princess to get everything you want out of life. In fact, being a princess requires that you wait for someone else to give you what you need—or, even worse, what they *think* you need. On the other hand, if you are ready and willing to take charge of your life, you get to be the author and master of your own story. Your reclamation has begun. Read on.

10

TURNING THE FAIRY TALE
INTO YOUR REALITY TALE

"Unpeel your dream from the center where it lives.
Step inside and begin living it."

—SARK, *Succulent Wild Woman*

FOR THIS CHAPTER you are going to need a notebook or
binder to keep all of your "work" together. I'm going to
present sixteen exercises to help you write your reality tale.
Each exercise will be like a brick in the foundation of the
reclaimed you that you are creating. We will keep working
until you have what you need to complete the reclamation
project. My reclamation book is a 9×12 sketchbook that
I purchased at a local art store. It has one hundred blank
perforated sheets. I got the perforated type because with
this project you should have the option of keeping what
empowers you and discarding what does not. So, should
you do an exercise that you do not want to see again, perhaps because it stirs up painful past memories, you can
simply tear it out and shred it (my favorite way to get rid of
paper) or burn it.

The amount of time you spend on your reclamation will
depend on how urgent this project feels for you, how much

time you have available, and your tolerance level for some of the surprising and even unsettling things this work may reveal about you. If you are like me—busy, a mom with lots of family obligations, and on the go much of the time—you might want to reserve a bit of time at the end of each day and do one or two exercises at a time. We are not out to break any speed records here. You can also take the "work" with you for stolen moments while your kids are at soccer practice, or the dentist's office.

The Past

Because so much of the sting of Powerful Mate Syndrome comes from past experiences, mental programming, and memories of the past, we are going to venture back into your history and work our way up to the present. The past has a hold on you whether you are conscious of it or not, and you simply cannot move forward until you have freed yourself from its grasp.

The purpose of the first few exercises is to get you conscious of the origins of your PMS. The remainder will focus on the future.

EXERCISE ONE: NAME THE CONTRIBUTORS

Make a list of all the people and things that might have contributed to your Powerful Mate Syndrome, either wittingly or unwittingly. The list does not have to contain specific names, but it can if you want to use them. You may be as general or specific as you like. The list is limited only by your thoughts. For example, your list might look similar to this:

1. My mother, who was the quintessential princess herself.

2. My father, who was the quintessential prince.

3. My grandparents, who believed in fairy tales.

4. Many of my teachers in high school.

5. The movies that make being a princess look so desirable.

6. Women who are hard-core traditionalists.

7. My boyfriend.

8. The authority figures in my childhood church.

9. My current partner.

Exercise Two: Write Each of Them a Letter

Take each person or item that you listed in exercise one and write him/her/it a letter to explain how your life has been affected by the myth of the "Powerful Prince" and "Princess" and what their role in it was. *You do not have to send the letter*, so be brutally honest. Use as little or as much space as you need to express your thoughts and feelings. This is your time to purge, vent, and let go of any pent-up emotions you have about that person and their connection to your Powerful Mate Syndrome. If you feel angry, sad, betrayed, or any other emotion, write it down. It might take one paragraph or several pages to complete this task. The object of the exercise is to shed light on PMS's existence in your life. It is like lancing a boil so that it can begin to heal. This is only for your use, so be honest and thorough with your feelings.

EXERCISE THREE: NAME ITS OTHER VICTIMS

Make a list of all the people who have been adversely impacted by you having Powerful Mate Syndrome. There should be at least two people on your list: you and your current or past partner. But be inclusive. Make your list as long as it needs to be to make it complete.

For example, if children are part of your relationship with your powerful partner, they have not had the benefit of seeing you full of self-expression, fulfilled, and living up to your potential in many areas of your life. As a result, they have suffered along with you and your partner. Be sure to put them on your list.

EXERCISE FOUR: WRITE LETTERS OF ACKNOWLEDGMENT

Your task in this exercise is to write letters of acknowledgment, *not apology*, to all the people on your list in exercise number three. The letter to yourself is to help you realize once and for all that you succumbed to PMS because of forces and influences that were not of your choosing or within your power to control. The letter to your spouse—current or former—is to acknowledge how you put the responsibility for your life and happiness on him and to release him from having to be "the prince." (You see, one of the things you are doing is freeing him to be himself.) As is the case in exercise two, you do not have to share these letters with anyone if you choose not to. Writing them is enough! Doing this with sincerity and integrity will thrust you forward exponentially in your battle to overcome Powerful Mate Syndrome.

The Present

Exercise Five: The Ten Qualities of My Princess

What is a princess? Make a list of ten words or characteristics that describe your idea of a princess. This is what my list looked like:

1. Helpless

2. Downtrodden

3. Not taken seriously

4. Fragile

5. Unfulfilled

6. Sedentary

7. Afraid

8. Dependent

9. Not very intelligent

10. Unhappy

EXERCISE SIX: IS SHE EMPOWERED OR IMPAIRED?

Go back to the ten things you wrote down in exercise number five. Next to each one write either EMPOWERED or IMPAIRED for the way you think it acts upon your psyche as you attempt to reclaim your personhood. For example, I would ask myself, "Does feeling helpless make me feel empowered or impaired as I move toward discarding PMS from my life?" Every one of the words on your list might not be negative. Go with whatever comes up for you. If you have words that make you feel empowered, then you are probably a little further along than many in your evolution from princess to woman of strength and purpose.

EXERCISE SEVEN: FROM IMPAIRED TO EMPOWERED

Take every "impaired" word from exercise six and replace it with a word or characteristic that gives you a sense of empowerment. Some of the words that might come to mind are:

powerful	active
independent	happy
confident	respected
needed	fulfilled
strong	challenged
courageous	empowered
useful	alive
beautiful	at peace
smart	in control

EXERCISE EIGHT: PURGING THE "POWERFUL PRINCE" FROM YOUR PSYCHE

In order to triumph over PMS you must discard the notion of "the Powerful Prince." Your partner has the right to be who he is without the expectation that he will live up to an unattainable standard set by a fairy tale. What expectations did you have of your partner that were based in fantasy? Write them all down. Don't hold back. When you are finished writing you have three choices: You can keep them to yourself, share them with your partner, or destroy them. It is entirely up to you.

EXERCISE NINE: UNDERSTANDING THE PAYOFF

What has been the payoff for you for being a princess? Did you get your needs met? Use as much space as you need and be brutally honest with your answers.

Exercise Ten: Calculating the Cost

What has being a princess cost you? Which of your needs did not get met? Use as much space as you need and be brutally honest with your answers.

Exercise Eleven: What Would I Have to Give Up?

Now write down your answer to the question: What would I have to give up to rid myself of Powerful Mate Syndrome? This question does not apply to material things, although if they occur to you, write them down. Write your ideas in complete sentences so that you get the declarative nature of what you are writing. There are no right or wrong answers. You should express your thoughts as thoroughly as possible. Some examples:

1. I would have to give up the false sense of security that being a princess creates.

2. I would have to give up making other people responsible for my happiness.

3. I would have to give up my expectation that marriage is always fun.

4. I would have to give up my denial of what my relationship is really like.

5. I would have to give up my picture of myself as a victim of circumstances beyond my control.

6. I would have to give up my naiveté about money.

7. I would have to give up believing that having money and happiness are the same thing.

8. I would have to give up my arrogance.

9. I would have to give up my know-it-all attitude.

10. I would have to give up telling myself that nothing in my past relationships has an effect on my current one.

EXERCISE TWELVE: IF I WEREN'T A PRINCESS, HOW WOULD MY LIFE BE DIFFERENT?

Write down your answer to these questions: How would my life be different if I went from being a princess to being a woman with strength and purpose in my relationship and my life? How would that difference show up in my life? Jot down everything that comes to mind. Then evaluate whether the differences are likely to be real or imagined. Some ideas that come to mind are:

1. I would take the initiative to plan some of the things I would like for my partner and me to do together instead of always waiting for him to do it.

2. I would check into the requirements for being a (firefighter, for example) even though it is a dangerous job.

3. I would be more assertive sexually with my partner.

4. I would stop worrying so much about looking like a fashion model and start acting like a role model.

5. I would start reading the financial section of the newspaper more often.

6. I would know what was in our household/business accounts and stop wondering if checks are going to bounce.

7. I would tell my partner how much I really *like* him, not just love him.

8. I would buy that Harley-Davidson motorcycle I've been dreaming of owning.

9. I would call a therapist without feeling ashamed, embarrassed, or weak for seeking help.

10. I would stop wallowing in my own self-pity, get off my derriere, and go create a life I loved.

11. I would create art and display it where everyone who came to my house could see it.

12. I would stop being afraid to go to the movies or to eat out alone.

13. I would sing in a karaoke bar even if I sounded terrible.

14. I would refuse to ride in the car with my partner when he drinks and drives.

15. I would write my Last Will and Testament.

16. I would insure my life.

17. I would buy myself beautiful lingerie, not for my mate, but for ME!

18. I could shop for the things my family needs and wants, not to fill a hole in my soul.

19. I could start shedding tears of joy instead of tears of sorrow.

20. I could see my partner as the person he really is rather than a mythical figure.

21. I could appreciate my partner's foibles as easily as his "fabulosity" (that's a Bette Midler term!).

22. I could finally see myself as a glorious, gifted, and generous person.

23. My heart could beat without aching.

After you have completed each of the preceding twelve exercises, you should be able to see clearly where you have given up your power in your relationship. You did not get to this place with the wave of a magic wand, and you cannot reverse it that way either. You should know without a doubt that you cannot change the way that you are in your relationship without changing the dynamics of the relationship with your partner. One part cannot change without affecting all the others. So what do you do with the information that you have garnered so far? Let's move into putting it to work.

The Future

Exercise Thirteen: Ten Things I'd Like to Change

Make a list of ten things that you haven't done because of your subordination to your mate. The purpose of this is not to find fault with you or to assign blame to anyone else, so include even the most minute thing that occurs to you. What dreams or goals have you given up along the way because you didn't think your spouse would approve? How many things did you not do for yourself because you thought they were your partner's responsibility? What were they? They might be things within your relationship, your career goals, and dreams for your life. Some examples are:

1. I failed to put myself in an environment that was intellectually stimulating.

2. I settle for being comfortable rather than challenged in almost every area of my life.

3. I never lived on my own.

4. I never moved to any place different after my early twenties.

5. I seldom, if ever, acknowledged the good things about my partner.

Exercise Fourteen: Your Game Plan

Of the ten things that you wrote down in exercise thirteen, are any of them goals that are still important for you to complete, attain, or attempt? Take each one that is still important to you and write out why. Then list the things you would need to do to bring it into fruition within a time frame that is acceptable to you. Not every item will take the same amount of time or attention. This exercise will help you figure out what will be required for each one. Be sure to ask yourself if it is something that you can do alone or whether you will need to enlist the help of others. This is your reclamation **game plan** for reclaiming your power and strength. (If you like, review chapter 6 about the power of having a game plan.) You may want to use a separate page for each item.

Working Your Reclamation Game Plan

Because PMS has more to do with yourself than with your mate, the work has to begin with you. Just like anything else worth having in life, reclaiming your strength and purpose may push you to your limit at times. But, if you keep your eyes on the prize, you can Proceed and Prevail. Every week you will take one item from exercise number fourteen and work your plan.

For example, if you wrote, "I loved to paint but gave it up

because I didn't get the encouragement of my spouse," then your plan might look like this:

The Task: Complete and show a painting to a trusted friend.

Time Frame: Six weeks.

Priorities: Set up a space in home where my materials won't be bothered. Make time on a regular basis to paint. Purchase easel and art supplies. Communicate with my spouse about my intention to pursue this activity. Look for a class to take once or twice a week to sharpen skills. Start talking to people in the local community about shows at street festivals, markets, etc.

Support Needed: I would like to have the support of my spouse but I will not let his lack of support stop my pursuit of this goal.

Commitment: Three times a week minimum.

Possible Obstacles: I may become afraid of my work being criticized by others. Lack of time, Lack of energy, lack of belief in myself.

Whenever thoughts pop into your head that you are not capable of achieving, whatever it is that you are attempting, I want you to say out loud to yourself:

I release the fairy tale, I embrace my power,
and I create my own reality tale.

You may find that you are talking to yourself constantly, but if that is what it takes to make it stick in your psyche, then that is what you will have to do. When I want to create a new permanent file in my mind's hard drive, I write it on Post-it notes and put them on my bathroom mirror, near my computer, on the refrigerator door, or anywhere else that I find myself with some frequency. It is amazing how quickly the concept becomes second nature. Try it.

Continue to do this each week with a new item on your list. Sometimes you will be working concurrently on more than one. That is fine as long as you do not become overwhelmed. If you do, slow down and complete one item before you proceed to the next. The goal is to make steady progress, not to set yourself up to feel like you failed.

Record your daily thoughts about your experiences in your reclamation journal. When you complete the first ten items on your game plan, go back and repeat the process as many times as necessary to make you feel complete with the past; done with being a princess. It is important to keep in mind that letting go of the princess is not synonymous with ending your relationship. With focus and effort, Powerful Mate Syndrome can be overcome.

Redefining Your Relationship

If you are still involved with your powerful partner, you will have to redefine that relationship. To some extent it's undoubtedly already happening. You are no longer the person you were, and your partner is bound to notice. Don't be surprised if he begins to look at you differently, perhaps even somewhat suspiciously. He is probably wondering who this newly empowered woman in his life is and where she came from. He may not have seen you so vital, vibrant, and in control of your own destiny since the early days of your relationship.

He may feel like he is living with a stranger. In some

ways, he is right. If you have relied on him for your sense of identity in the past but are now taking responsibility for yourself, you are indeed a new person. If you are taking the reins of your development and growth rather than neglecting them, these may also seem to be the actions of a stranger. Without you having to say a word, he will know that something is in the air. But you don't want to leave him wondering or guessing.

Ironically, your partner may be more welcoming of this change than you imagined. Part of taking back the responsibility for your own life means liberating him from the burden of responsibility for it. He will most likely find that your decision and action to embrace your power and regain your strength and purpose takes a tremendous weight off of his shoulders.

You must do the work, but you don't want to do it without being fully connected and engaged with your partner. After all, Powerful Mate Syndrome exists only in the presence of a partner whom the woman deems powerful, so he's been a part of the picture from the very beginning, regardless of whether he knows that or not. When you disconnect from the fairy tale, you make room for your authentic mate to show up, taking the place of the mythic prince who can restore life, move mountains, and heal the world with a single kiss.

To stay connected while embracing change is a tall order. But it is also doable. If ever there was a time when good listening and communication skills were assets, this is it. Be open to questions your partner might have. Welcome the opportunity to engage in conversation at all times. Your partner will experience various emotions ranging from curiosity and excitement to loss and grief. Why grief, you might ask? Because any time something ends there is a loss. Even if it is the retiring of an old, ineffective way of being in your relationship, it is still a loss and needs to be acknowledged before you can both move on to the next phase of your relationship.

It's normal to be apprehensive, even afraid, about your spouse's reaction; any time there is change in a family system, there is usually an accompanying fear. But you can't let fear stop you. Remember, if you find yourself feeling afraid, you can always say to yourself and say often:

"I release the fairy tale, I embrace my power, and I create my own reality tale."

There is a concept in psychology that says whenever the member of a family who has played the role of "the sick one" begins to become well, someone else in the family begins to take that person's place and starts to exhibit signs of "sickness." The purpose of being connected and making communication a priority is to eliminate the need of a role for "the sick one" in the family altogether. We do not want to take two steps forward and three steps back. No— Proceed and Prevail is our motto and our intention! Now, get out your reclamation journals and complete the following exercises.

EXERCISE FIFTEEN: TEN WORDS FOR CONNECTED

Make a list of ten words to describe the way you feel when you are connected to and communicating with your partner without the cloud of Powerful Mate Syndrome over your relationship.

Exercise Sixteen: Describing the Difference

Describe the difference in your relationship between when you were totally immersed in PMS and now. Do you feel that you have completely excised it from your psyche, or do remnants of it still exist? Explain your feelings in your journal. Use as much time and space as you need. Remember, this is only for your use. However, if you are feeling a high level of connection with your partner, feel free to share this exercise with him. Invite him to share his feelings about the difference in your relationship from his perspective. Listen to what he has to say without judgment or criticism. Keep the dialogue open so that your connection to each other will remain strong.

Above all, remember this: Redefining your relationship will take time and patience. It may be that you and your partner find that you need to improve your communication skills to help you accomplish redefining your relationship. Let me caution you against trying to "do therapy" on your mate. This is a process that is ongoing; if you need the help of a therapist or other qualified practitioner, don't hesitate to get that help. Marshal every resource available to make your relationship strong, resilient, stimulating, and fulfilling— for both of you. Redefining your relationship will open the door to many new possibilities, some of which neither you nor your partner will have ever dreamed possible because you were stuck in the fairy tale. You have permission to release the fairy tale and to embrace the joys and possibilities that lie ahead.

The Final Chapter: Writing Your Reality Tale

You have taken a long journey. You are to be commended for facing the ugly truth about Powerful Mate Syndrome and for taking the steps necessary to break free once and for all. The first step is awareness. The second is action. The result of the two will be a new chapter in your life—your reality tale—and *you* get to be its primary author. Of course, your powerful partner, recently liberated from his own psychological prison of princedom, will help you as coauthor.

The beauty of releasing the fairy tale and embracing your own power is that you can create whatever it is in your story that delights you. You no longer need to follow someone else's script—whether the writer existed centuries ago in a land "far far away" or as nearby as the person you share a life and home with. No longer do you need to believe that you have to choose between being fulfilled and being loved. Now you know that *you don't have to be less of who you are in an attempt to make your partner more of who he is.* You've been enlightened, educated, and empowered to create your own reality tale.

The fairy tales about the prince and damsel in distress in need of rescue will continue to be disseminated through novels, magazines, television shows, and in movies. Females of all ages will continue to be bombarded by the message that they need to be rescued and taken care of by a powerful partner. But those of us who have suffered in silence for too long now know how to help ourselves.

Here's to your reality tale, complete with its very own happy ending. Proceed and Prevail!

ACKNOWLEDGMENTS

Once upon a time there was a woman who had an idea for a book, but that was all she had. Well, actually, she had an idea and the belief that it needed to be shared with others. She had very little knowledge about the realities of writing a book, much less getting one published. Nevertheless, she began to write down her thoughts, filling one legal pad after another. Soon she had so many pads that she needed a more efficient way to store her work. She decided to buy a laptop computer and it became her constant companion. But one day tragedy struck. Her companion's hard drive crashed and she feared that everything would be irretrievably lost. But two knights, Shahrokh and Ben at Computer Boy in Los Angeles, recovered the data and saved the day! Actually they saved the book! The woman was so grateful and continued on her journey.

The journey was long. Along the way she met angels, knights, queens, kings, and all kinds of well-wishers and helpers. There was Andrea Henkart, a warm and generous soul who shared information and gave her much guidance. Then there was Mark Steisel and Ramon Williamson, two more angels who helped her tremendously. A few more months into the journey she came upon a king and a queen, though not married to one another, named Joel Roberts and Bonnie Grey from Joel Roberts and Associates. Their media training and encouragement breathed new life into the woman, who was beginning to feel tired and losing hope that someone might want her book.

It was Joel who made one telephone call that resulted in numerous television and radio interviews for the woman. And then out of nowhere the miracles began to fall upon her like raindrops in the spring. An angel named Marian Lizzi, the woman who would eventually become the woman's editor at St. Martin's Press, appeared and, without any prior knowledge of the woman with the book, decided to take a chance on her. By now the woman had begun to assemble the circle of people that she would need to make the book a reality. Watching out for her at every turn were her literary agents, Greg Dinkin and Frank Scatoni of Venture Literary. They were knights in shining armor (regular men's clothing, actually) and they took up her cause and charged into battle on her behalf. Now the woman was no longer alone, fending off criticism, doubt, and rejection. She had trusted companions on the journey.

The woman and her cast of characters felt that something was missing—that they needed help from someone special to bring the book to fruition. It wasn't long before they met up with Caroline Pincus, who calls herself a book midwife. Caroline was the missing piece, and along she came on the journey, bringing her extraordinary skills as a writer, editor, collaborator, and understanding coach. She became a trusted member of the woman's inner circle, and just as her moniker says, she helped the woman bring the book, *Powerful Mate Syndrome,* to life. And so, what started out as a bunch of ideas scribbled on notepads evolved into the book you are holding in your hands.

There were many others who contributed to the woman in one way or another during this nearly five-year journey. Dr. Judith Bin-Nun, Dr. Toby Bobes, and Carol Hayman, each accomplished practitioners in the field of psychology, helped the woman through some of the most daunting stretches of the journey. The stellar instructors at Antioch University, Los Angeles, are all represented in this book in one way or another.

And then there are the angels and helpers, coaches and confidantes without whom this journey could not have been completed. First there is the woman's brother, Anthony, who sent constant waves of love and dry humor via e-mail and telephone. He's simply the best brother a woman could have. Arthur Jenkins, musician extraordinaire but, more important, a member of the woman's family, provided beautiful music for her to listen to while she wrote and was always ready with copious words of encouragement. Paula Brown, an angel with the biggest heart I've ever seen, was taking the journey along with the woman long before the idea for the book was conceived. She redefines the meaning of the word *friend.* Margaret "Beautiful" Pazant is a spiritual coach and angel that helped the woman "take her life back" in 1994 and has been a steadfast friend ever since. When she felt she had no more to give, "Beautiful" was there to help her summon her strength and carry on. Another of the woman's longtime friends and allies, Venus Thomas, also supported, encouraged, and buoyed her as she made her way through the unfamiliar and oftentimes baffling literary world.

There were far too many others who contributed their love, generosity, warm wishes, and encouragement to the woman, and space constraints make it impossible to list every one of their names. Nevertheless, there are some that must be acknowledged by name to convey the woman's overwhelming gratitude. Of course there are the creative and talented people at St. Martin's Press that made this book a reality, including Sheila Curry Oakes, Julie Mente, Joan Higgins, and many others whose names will probably never be known. Thank you one and all. Diane Margolin, the editor and publisher of the *Santa Monica Star* newspaper, gave the woman an opportunity to write and express her feelings in print before anyone else. Thank you. The woman wishes to extend much gratitude for the tape that Matt Radecki at Bouquet Media made, which opened so many doors of opportunity. And then there is the incredible circle of friends and soul mates to whom the woman is eternally grateful. Some of them are Sari Ehrenriech, Tammy Andrews, Valerie Heine, Patricia Jackson Woolridge, Diane Chavez, Carol Stevens, Raul, Vicki and Julia Dominguez, Liza Wachter, Kathie Johnson, Irma Hopkins, Dr. Ken Mask, Rochelle Robertson, Julianne Hinton, Michael Shea, "Dame" Judy Harris, Steve "Rosy" Rosen, Steve and Susan Hoch, Dr. Robert Paoletti, Constance Dennerline, Susan Birrell, Dr. Ileana Zapatero, Barbara "Babs" Allen, Jon and Jane Broderud, Elizabeth Mullan, and Penny Wineberg. To all of you and to those whose names may have escaped me in this moment, thank you for accompanying me on this incredible journey.

FURTHER READING
AND RESOURCES

BOOKS

Bach, David. *Smart Women Finish Rich* (New York: Broadway Books, 1999).

Ban Breathnach, Sarah. *Simple Abundance: A Daybook of Comfort and Joy* (New York: Warner Books, 1995).

————. *Something More: Excavating Your Authentic Self* (New York: Warner Books, 1998).

Barrett, Marilyn. *Just Sign Here, Honey: Women's 10 Biggest Legal Mistakes & How to Avoid Them* (Capital Books, Inc., 2003).

Beattie, Melody. *The Language of Letting Go* (Center City, Minn.: Hazelden Foundation, 1990).

Dubin, Arlene G. *Prenups for Lovers: A Romantic Guide to Prenuptial Agreements* (New York: Random House, 2001).

Godfrey, Neale S. *Making Change: A Woman's Guide to Designing Her Financial Future* (New York: Simon & Schuster, 1997).

Hammerslough, Jane. *Dematerializing: Taming the Power of Possessions* (Cambridge, Mass.: Perseus Publishing, 2001).

Hayes, Christopher L., and Kate Kelly. *Money Makeovers: How Women*

Can Control Their Financial Destiny (New York: Main Street Books, 1999).

Holmes, Ernest. *This Thing Called You* (New York: Jeremy P. Tarcher/ Putnam, 1997).

James, Jennifer. *Success is the Quality of Your Journey* (New York: Newmarket Press, 1983).

Lerner, Harriet. *The Dance of Anger* (New York: Harper & Row, 1985).

———. *The Dance of Deception* (New York: HarperCollins, 1993).

———. *The Dance of Intimacy* (New York: Harper & Row, 1989).

Orman, Suze. *The Courage to be Rich* (New York: Riverhead Books, 1999).

———. *The Road to Wealth* (New York: Riverhead Books, 2001).

Paul, Jordan, and Margaret Paul. *Do I Have To Give Up Me To Be Loved By You?* (Minneapolis: CompCare, 1983).

Reilly, Patricia Lynn. *Imagine A Woman in Love with Herself* (Berkeley, Calif.: Conari Press, 1999).

Richardson, Cheryl. *Take Time for Your Life* (New York: Broadway Books, 1999).

Sark, *Succulent Wild Woman* (New York: Fireside, 1997).

Shriver, Maria. *Ten Things I Wish I'd Known* (New York: Warner Books, 2000).

Viorst, Judith. *Necessary Losses* (New York: Fireside, 1986).

Ward, Francine. *Esteemable Acts* (New York: Broadway Books, 2003).

Wilde, Stuart. *The Trick to Money Is Having Some* (Carlsbad, Calif.: Hay House, 1989).

Williamson, Marianne. *A Woman's Worth* (New York: Random House, 1993).

WEB SITES

www.bankrate.com/brm/prenup.asp
www.beingmindful.com
www.blackwomenshealth.com
www.equalityinmarriage.org
www.fool.com

www.getmentalhelp.com

www.gettingremarried.com/prenuptial_agreement.
 html

www.ivillage.com

www.mental-health-matters.com

www.ndvh.org (The National Domestic Violence Hotline
 Web site)

www.self-esteem-nase.org

www.wealthywomen.org

www.womenof.com/articles/le031297.asp

INDEX

Clinton, Hillary, 173
communication
    game plan, 140, 154–155
    prenuptial agreement, 166–169
    sex appeal and, 118
community leaders, power sources,
    49–50
confidentiality, xi
Congreve, William, 112
counseling. *See* couples counseling
couples counseling, 112–134
    beliefs revealed by, 131–134
    benefits of, 113–114
    cautionary scenarios, 123–128
    cultural factors, 120
    expectations of, 120–121
    frequency of sessions, 113
    importance of, 112–113
    marital, 130
    premarital, 128–130
    referral sources, 121–122
    selection of counselor, 118–120
    stigma and, 115
credentials, of couples counselor,
    119
credit, establishment of, 189–191
cultural factors, couples counseling,
    120

death, identity loss, 66–72
dependence, gender roles,
    17–18
desertion, identity loss, 66–72
Diana (princess of Wales), 37
divorce
    identity loss, 66–72
    prenuptial agreement, 159,
        176–177

domestic violence
    game plan, 142
    money, 186–188
dreams. *See* career goals

emotional isolation, Powerful Mate
    Syndrome, 20
employment, money, 188–189
empowerment, impairment and,
    207–209
endings, 103–111
    inevitability of, 103–105
    might have beens, 109–110
    Powerful Mate Syndrome,
        107–109
    prenuptial agreement, 158
    proactive responses, 110–111
    reality and, 105–106
    romance, 103
engagement. *See also* endings;
    marriage; premarital
    considerations; prenuptial
    agreement
    arrogance and, 114
    couples counseling, 128–130
    endings, 103–111
    game plan, 137
    importance of, 116–118
    prenuptial agreement,
        161–162
ethics, couples counseling, 120
extended family
    game plan, 141–142
    prenuptial agreement, 164

fame
    endings, 107–109
    power sources, 43–48

WHAT'S YOUR STORY?

I am putting together an anthology of stories by and about women who have overcome Powerful Mate Syndrome. If you or someone you know has a story you want to share, please send it to me:

> Angela Wilder
> Powerful Mate Syndrome Stories
> 15237 Sunset Blvd., #86
> Pacific Palisades, CA 90272

or e-mail me at powerfulmates@aol.com.

Please indicate how or if you would like to be credited. If your story is chosen for the collection, I will be sure that you are credited properly or your anonymity protected, as you wish. Thank you!